The Perfect World
Inside my Minivan

One mom's journey through the streets of suburbia

Marybeth Hicks

faith
publishing service
books

www.faithpublishingservice.com

International Standard Book Number (10): 0-9790747-0-3
International Standard Book Number (13): 978-0-9790747-0-7

Library of Congress Control Number: 2006910027

Cover and text design by Enomhen Odigie and Abby Wieber,
Faith Publishing Service

Illustrations by David Clark
www.clarktoon.com

Distributed by University of Chicago Press, 427 E. 60th Street Chicago, IL 60637

Printed and bound in the United States of America.

With love and thanks to
Katie, Betsy, Jimmy and Amy
for letting me share you with the world...
and especially to Jim
for sharing the world with me.

Foreword

I have spent almost half of my 20 years in journalism helping parents navigate the rough waters of our culture. Believe me, it's a lonely battle. Sometimes it feels as though I'm a salmon swimming against the strong current of what's popular and easy.

Is not enough that our society doesn't help us, it actually works against the values of most parents. Sadly, many parents are abdicating their roles and letting society raise their kids. Yet, others are not giving up the fight.

Marybeth Hicks is one such parent. When Marybeth came to my office at *The Washington Times* to pitch her column *Then Again,* I thought: "Thank you, dear Lord. The angels have sent me a kindred spirit – a fellow soldier in this culture war."

Marybeth's writing was clear, passionate and written as a parent who understood the high stakes involved in raising tomorrow's generation. I felt fortunate to have her write a weekly column for our Family Times section. Her work is so important that it runs on the cover, along with a color illustration.

As a loving wife and mother of four, Marybeth reports from the front line, the trenches of family life. She speaks with the authority of a parent who has stayed awake worrying about a sick child, wiped the tears away from a little daughter whose best friend moved away, held the hand of a timid teenager who feared not measuring up to the "in" crowd, demonstrated integrity to children who are learning to be young men and women.

Marybeth gets it.

She knows that parenting, the hardest and most rewarding job available, is about molding future generations, teaching them right from wrong, inspiring them to be the best men and women they can be – and improving ourselves in the process.

It's not easy. Sometimes you have to be the "meanie" and say no, so children don't learn the wrong lessons.

There have been times when I've been so touched by her columns that I've cried. There have been times when I have joined her in indignation when she's pointed out an injustice. There've been times when I've laughed out loud at her anecdotes, shaking my head and agreeing with her as someone who's been there and done that. And there have been times when I've sat quietly and reflected deeply on what she's written.

Her columns hit you right in the heart.

I hope you enjoy reading these columns as much as I have enjoyed editing them. They are a treasure. I've been honored to be her editor and consider myself privileged to have her friendship.

Maria Stainer
Assistant Managing Editor - Features and Culture
The Washington Times
Washington, D.C.

Foreword

As the pastor of a Catholic parish, I sometimes feel as if I experience a tiny fraction of what it is like to be a parent. Like a parent, I am part of the joy, the grief, the tears and celebrations of my parish family. Like a parent, I listen to their hopes, sorrows and plans for the future. During my time as pastor, I have come to deeply appreciate the struggles and sacrifices made by so many parents. I congratulate them for their tenacity, patience and grace under pressure.

Marybeth Hicks is writing for all those parents – and for everyone who experiences family life. When I read Marybeth's musings on her child-rearing journey, I often laugh out loud – and just as often find myself pondering some nugget of wisdom lurking in the humor. Marybeth's view from her mini-van is a clear-eyed, common-sense and humorous look at the ups and downs of being a mom – or a dad.

As the editor of FAITH Publishing Service, I have been proud to feature Marybeth's column in our magazine each month – and I am now enormously proud to be part of publishing this, her first book.

Father Dwight Ezop
Editor-in-Chief
Faith Publishing Service
Lansing, Michigan

Introduction

A young mom I know says of her life, "The hours drag so slowly but the years fly by."

If ever you want to experience this phenomenon, I'd encourage you to write a newspaper column about your children. There are days when my kids are at school and the hours from 8 a.m. until 3 p.m. are filled only with deafening, seemingly endless silence – which coincidentally is the sound of a writer who can't think of anything to write. Yet the years since I started to chronicle my motherhood journey have passed in the blink of an eye, a fact that frequently causes mine to mist.

When I launched *Then again…*, Katie was a high school freshman and Amy was a first grader; Betsy and Jimmy fit neatly in between. I was still driving all four children through the streets of suburbia, ferrying and parenting from season to season.

But like my young friends says, the years do fly.

As an example, consider that my first column for *The Washington Times* entitled "Nobody warned me about driver's ed," contemplated the upcoming year in which my daughter would hold a learner's permit. Since then I've written two more pieces about Katie and cars – one about the vehicle we purchased for her use, and another about the accident in which she totaled it (all three columns are included in this collection).

These days I spend less time in the van but more money on gas (for the replacement third car). The prospect of sending Katie off to college looms ahead in a matter of months, bringing with it the poignant reality that while the journey of motherhood lasts forever, it also is ironically fleeting.

Of course, no mother journeys alone. I'm fortunate to share the ride with a spectacular husband and father. Jim isn't always mentioned in my column, but make no mistake – his insights and influence are there between each and every line. My sister Ellen Campbell and sister-in-law Catherine Brennan are the "emergency moms" on the form at my kids' schools, and also in my heart. The rest of my siblings and their families, as well as a core group of incredible friends, round out the "village" in which I am thankful to be raising my children.

I've also had great company on my writer's journey. In particular my parents, Polly and Tom Brennan, have offered unwavering support since I first called and asked if I could read columns to them over the phone back in January 2004. With their encouragement, I screwed up the nerve to send a query to Maria Stainer, assistant managing editor of *The Washington Times*. Maria gave me the one thing every writer must have to succeed: A chance. I remain unspeakably grateful to her.

Along my path, I've been mentored and promoted by some fine, fine people. Faith Publishing Services President Patrick O'Brien, *FAITH Magazine* Editor-in-Chief Fr. Dwight Ezop and Editorial Director Elizabeth Solsburg have supported me with regular freelance work and a place for Michigan readers to enjoy *Then again...* (and thanks to them you hold this book in your hands!). I'm proud to be on the pages of *FAITH Magazine* and especially honored to help launch a new line of books from FAITH Publishing Service.

I'm indebted as well to Binyamin Jolkovsky, Jen Singer, Lisa Hendey, Lisa Wheeler, Josh Raymond, Sean Harriott, Tim Bete, and Fr. Charlie Irvin.

The best compliment I get on any column is when someone says, "I felt you somehow gained access to my minivan and hid in the rear seat taking notes about our family." Telling my own parenting stories seems to give a voice to other moms and dads, whose lives are packed with the precious – sometimes overwhelming – but always entertaining experiences of family life.

I hope this collection of columns feels fun and familiar. As for me, I only wish it wouldn't go by so quickly.

Marybeth Hicks
October 2006
East Lansing, Michigan

Table of Contents

1 The perfect world inside my minivan

39 Bringing up geeks

Nobody warned me about driver's ed

'The talk' is not a one-time event

Einstein's mother's theory of relativity

Let the boredom begin

Marybeth Hicks

The perfect world inside my minivan

Marybeth Hicks

The perfect world inside my minivan

I t wasn't really a gift – or even a surprise – but the Honda dealer put a giant red bow on the rearview mirror anyway.

Perhaps because my husband picked up the van without me in the week before Christmas, the staff figured he was playing Santa Claus. We don't have the kind of marriage – financially or otherwise – that allows for clandestine purchases of vehicles, so I knew it was coming. Still, the bow was a nice touch.

That was more than six years and 150,000 miles ago. I'm recalling the bow and the newness it once represented as I stand in a puddle at the "touch free" car wash, waiting for a young man in wet sneakers to clean one of the cup holders – for a second time. The first time, he left the sticky brown residue of chocolate milk in a perfect dried circle at the bottom of the vinyl well.

"Who had chocolate milk in the van?" I wonder. Probably the same person who left an unopened but crumbled package of cheese and crackers in the seat pocket.

I spent the first 10 minutes at the car wash off-loading trash – crusts of peanut-butter toast from the passenger door's storage compartment, gum wrappers, two travel mugs, two eraser tips, a copy of Agatha Christie's "Murder on the Orient Express" (not trash, just abandoned), a section of old newspaper, a collection of ponytail holders. At least this time there are no dirty socks.

Every so often, I land here in the deluxe car wash to reclaim my van from the clutches of life with four children. When I do, I promise myself that it's going to stay clean for a while.

"A while" is roughly three days.

I hadn't realized before children that in addition to wreaking havoc on my sleeping patterns and our joint checking account, they would transform my vehicle from a tidy transportation system into a mobile snack-center/locker-room/confessional. My van fills more roles than the Batmobile – though it doesn't float or fly, which sometimes would be helpful.

The change occurred, immediately, with the first child. One day I drove a pristine Honda Accord, and the next I realized its interior conveniently was the same color as old raisins, allowing them to blend into the carpet for weeks between visits to the

"U-Vac" auto center.

The plush interior inside my Honda couldn't hide the smell of sour milk, though. It's a smell mothers get used to eventually, but not everyone can control the gag reflex it induces. I once offered to drive my boss to lunch so we could continue a meeting while eating a burger. My car had warmed nicely while sitting in our sunny employee parking lot, heating my eldest daughter's lost baby bottle to a putrid, curdled stink.

Being both a mother and the owner of the car, I simply didn't notice it. I should have realized there was a problem when my boss put his head out the window for the entire ride to the restaurant. Usually particular about his hairstyle, he allowed his meticulous comb-over to blow wildly in the breeze while he gasped for air and shouted over his shoulder, "Can't you smell something?"

It took a few weeks, but I finally found a bottle wedged under the upholstery, forced there by the back edge of the car seat that marked me as a changed woman.

These days, I spend roughly a third of my day in my Odyssey minivan, a private office for parenting that holds 150,146 miles of secrets and tears, laughter and lessons.

It's where I first hear about long days at school or a lonely night at a dance. It holds gangs of friends on Halloween or a single, sad, homesick girl on her way back from a failed sleepover. It's the private space to explain a bad grade or a missed shot or a poor choice. It's familiar and safe, an extension of the home it finds almost by rote.

The dents and spots reveal my van's storied past. On the ceiling is a Diet Coke stain from a 2-liter bottle that rolled around undetected for a couple of days before exploding on the way to school; the bumper recalls the time I backed into a car parked at the bottom of my brother's driveway that belonged to a couple from China whose limited English did not include the words "no-fault insurance."

The car-wash staff gets impatient when I ask them to re-vacuum under the third seat. "I'm sorry, but for $25, I have to insist you actually clean the car," I say with a smile to hide my irritation. I've already put a tip in the jar, so I'm determined to get my money's worth.

Finally driving into the brilliant sunshine, I breathe in the "new car" air freshener I requested. In my perfect future, when my children are grown and gone and driving cars of their own, I'll cruise about town in a sporty sedan that smells new for as long as I keep it.

I'll never open a rear door and find a forgotten trombone, an assortment of colored pencils, a geometry book or a half-eaten bagel. My car again will be my personal domain, its interior reflecting my neat-freakish personality.

Until then, I guess I'll just enjoy the perfect world I'm in now, raisins and all.

Marybeth Hicks

Imagining Life as the worlds Best Mom

Her minivan turned out of the school parking lot and cruised gracefully down the street, sunlight streaming into her open window. The gentle breeze lifted her hair softly away from her face and twisted the several blue ribbons hanging from her rearview mirror.

How cute, I thought. She hangs her children's ribbons in her car. They must feel proud.

I approached the stop sign behind her and crept slowly toward her back bumper. That's when I saw it – the ribbon that told me everything I needed to know – the ribbon that proved I was (sort of) in the presence of greatness.

Its red letters were outlined in gold: "World's Best Mom."

There she was. I couldn't believe it. The world's best mom was driving the van right in front of me. She had just dropped her children at school, and now she must be headed home for a day of world-class motherhood.

For the rest of my drive home, I wondered what a day in the life of the world's best mom would be like.

The world's best mom probably would arrive back home and head straight to her children's rooms to make sure their beds were made and their pajamas were put away. She would rinse the toothpaste blobs out of the sink, open the shades and grab the laundry, smiling contentedly at the chocolate stains on her son's T-shirt as she thought of the fun they had had going out for ice cream the night before.

The world's best mom would get the washer and dryer going, pull a roast out of the freezer for dinner and then sit down in her sunny kitchen to plan the end-of-the-year party for her daughter's class. It would be so pleasant in her kitchen, what with the smell of brownies baking in the oven

She'd make a list of errands (buy teacher gifts, get new baseball gear for Junior, buy a birthday gift for Susie to take to a party, stop at the grocery store for vegetables that don't come in cans), and then maybe she'd make some phone calls to organize a Cub Scout camping trip.

The world's best mom might then walk the dog, put in an hour of yardwork, eat a healthy lunch and then head to the school to volunteer in the library.

I can just imagine how organized and productive the world's best mom is. She looks at her calendar and plans ahead. She's never caught off guard. Heck, she's the world's best.

I'm not the world's best mom.

When I get home from dropping my children at school, I have to tackle the war zone that is my kitchen. It takes a solid hour to empty and reload the dishwasher, sweep the Rice Krispies off the floor, wipe the syrup off the table from someone's frozen waffle breakfast (Note: The world's best mom would serve homemade) and refill the dog dish.

These chores are daunting, so instead, I usually just pour another cup of coffee and read the paper.

While the world's best mom makes sure in advance that her children have the perfect gifts for friends' birthday parties, I buy things en route. I thought this was the whole reason decorative gift bags were invented – for people like me who purchase presents at the pharmacy, along with a card, some tissue paper and a container in which to present the gift.

The world's best mom probably makes the world's best dinners. This is another way in which she and I are different, because I stand in front of the freezer at 6:45 every evening trying to figure out what to serve and calculating how long it takes to defrost and then cook different cuts of meat.

The world's best mom probably knows the rules to soccer, something I still can't figure out no matter how many games I attend.

She probably keeps photo albums chronicling the growth of her children from the days they were born (using acid-free photo paper so the pictures don't fade).

I bet the world's best mom finds time to play checkers with her children and always reads to them before bed, something she can do because she's not still doing dinner dishes at 8:30.

Those are the things I would do if I were the world's best mom, anyway.

For the record, when I had my first daughter, I meant to be the world's best mom, and with only one child, I did OK. Even when I had just two children, I was pretty good – though admittedly this was about the time when I started to make compromises (ready-to-bake cookies instead of dough from scratch, for example).

By the time I had three and then four children, it was painfully clear I wasn't ever going to achieve world-class status in the motherhood game. There were too many schedules to juggle, too many problems to solve, too few hours just to listen and talk.

I had no choice but to drop my standards and settle for something less – something like "World's Most Well-Intentioned Mom" or "World's Most Remorseful Mom."

Who would want a ribbon hanging from the rearview mirror to acknowledge such a status ?

Then again, though I know I'm not the world's best mom, I also know there are four children who seem to think I'm good enough, and that's even better than a ribbon (though a certificate would still be nice).

Marybeth Hicks

Once again, this mom doesn't get the picture

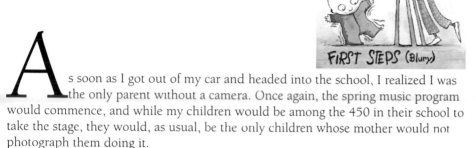

FIRST STEPS (Blury)

As soon as I got out of my car and headed into the school, I realized I was the only parent without a camera. Once again, the spring music program would commence, and while my children would be among the 450 in their school to take the stage, they would, as usual, be the only children whose mother would not photograph them doing it.

It's always the same. From the first day of the new school year right through the farewell picnic and Field Day, I never have a camera on hand. Or if I do remember to bring one, it's out of film, or its batteries are dead, or I leave it locked in the car.

When it comes to photos, I've concluded there are two kinds of parents: those who take pictures and those of us who ask other parents to snap pictures of our children and send the images to us if they get the chance.

Moreover, you're either a natural born "picture parent" or you're not.

From the beginning, my husband and I were overwhelmed by the prospect of photographing our first child. This might have had to do with the packet of new-parent information from the hospital where Katie was born. It offered a "newborn budget" to estimate the first-year expenses associated with our new bundle of joy. The list of items included diapers, baby toys, insurance and first-year photos. The estimated cost for pictures? $1,200.

Let me restate this in case you're not clear. The packet said we should plan to spend one-thousand-two-hundred dollars taking pictures of our daughter in her first year of life.

Right away, it was obvious we were going to fail this aspect of parenting. For one thing, we would have to choose between photographing our baby and feeding her, not to mention that that kind of financial burden would preclude any future siblings.

We took the obligatory snapshots as we left the hospital and then about 36 pictures of Katie as she slept. After that, it was spotty.

Neglecting to take early childhood photos can remain a dirty little secret. Once your child goes to school, however, everyone discovers you never take her picture. What's worse, there are so many opportunities to not take her picture. "Picture parents" record every Halloween parade, Christmas program, birthday party and band concert their child attends. I wouldn't be able to find the camera that many times in a year.

I suppose I might take pictures at these events, if I took pictures, but I asked myself at a DARE graduation, "If I take pictures right now, would I even know what event this was when I looked at the photos later?" I'd have to ask my son someday in the future, "Why were you sitting in the gym with all your friends listening to a police officer? What kind of trouble were you in?"

Some things are better lived than relived.

Instead, I take rolls and rolls of the same pose, in case the last shot didn't come out. Rather than a chronological account of our family's growth through the years, we have the pose at the river, the pose on the front porch and the pose in front of the Christmas tree. This is how we mark time.

One year, in an effort to redeem myself, I started a new role of 36 pictures on the first day of school and vowed to capture the highlights of every season. I caught the field trip to the apple orchard in September. I snapped pictures of my children trick-or-treating in October. I got shots of us gathered around the Thanksgiving turkey. I captured Christmas morning

Then spring came, and the camera malfunctioned, rewinding the film to the beginning. Because it looked as if I had a new role in the camera, I took pictures of the Valentine's party, St. Patrick's Day, First Communion and May crowning.

When I got the film developed, there were two images on every print – all 72 pictures for the academic year, neatly packaged on 36 blurry photos.

There were happy faces meshed on top of cheesy grins, good hair transposed over bad hair.

Were we smiling in this picture, or is that a turkey leg?

That was back when Katie was in the second grade. This week, she went to the junior prom, proving that time marches on even if you don't capture it on film.

Before the dance, Katie and her prom-going pals gathered with their parents for pictures at the home of one of the girls. Flashes popped while nervous teens held toothsome grins. My daughter and her friends looked picture-perfect, but did I have a camera?

No. I had a dead camera battery at the bottom of my purse to remind me what size battery to buy. Some things never change.

I thought about my photographically challenged parenting style as I enjoyed the spring concert at the elementary school. The third grade sang a charming piece – "The Pasta Song" – and my son's class sang *The Wreck of the Edmund Fitzgerald*.

I don't have any pictures of them, but that's OK. I know I won't forget the concert anytime soon.

I can't get the Edmund Fitzgerald song out of my head.

Marybeth Hicks

Research proves parents right

(but who's surprised?)

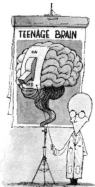

There is something parents of teenagers sometimes say when faced with the reckless, thoughtless and self-absorbed behavior of our offspring. It's perhaps not the kindest thing we could say, but it turns out it's entirely true. What we say is: "For crying out loud, why don't you use your brain?"

We pose this rhetorical question when our teens drive cars that have illuminated low-fuel warnings until the engine dies on the roadside or when they leave expensive miniature electronic devices in the pockets of bluejeans headed for the washer.

We ask this question when our teens succumb to peer pressure, or lead a group of friends into a dangerous situation. We always ask it when the police are involved.

And of course, it's the only thing to say when teens open their mouths and utter the unkind, insensitive yet routine comments for which adolescents are well known, such as, "You're such a jerk," "You're a moron," and "I hate you" (a comment made all the more hurtful by the sound of a slamming door).

Well, it turns out "Why don't you use your brain?" isn't just a belittling, sarcastic, frustrated expression of parental indignation.

Separate studies by researchers at both the National Institutes for Health and the University College of London prove what parents have known for generations. Teens don't use their brains.

Apparently, the part of the brain that inhibits risky behavior may not be fully developed until age 25. This explains the price of auto insurance.

In addition to lacking the brainpower to assess risk and act accordingly, the region of the brain associated with higher-level thinking – empathy, guilt and understanding the motivations of others – is underused by teenagers. Instead, teens rely on the posterior area of the brain – the part involved with perceiving and imagining actions.

So there it is. All this time we've been asking our teens "Why don't you use your brain?" and the answer they've been giving us – "Um... I don't know" – turns out to be true.

Research is good, and I want to be an enlightened parent, so I'm glad to know what I reasonably should expect from my children in each developmental stage. In fact, this has been my M.O. in parenting – finding out what's considered "normal" (give or take) and then setting my expectations accordingly.

I learned this strategy early in my parenting career. Katie, my oldest, was about two years old when my aunt came for a visit. Being a social worker and a mother of four, she was one of my role models and mentors in parenting. I was always eager to hear Aunt Mary's advice.

She watched Katie wandering around our back yard, eating dirt and sticking mulch in her ears (OK, I'm exaggerating about the mulch), and she said something I never forgot: "A two year old should behave a lot like a well-trained golden retriever. She should feed herself, nap frequently and come when she's called."

Katie didn't come when she was called, so my aunt's insight gave me something to work on.

The point is, understanding what you can reasonably expect from a child is a good way to set your standards for appropriate behavior.

But this leaves me with a bit of a dilemma.

On the one hand, current research shows adolescents aren't intentionally cruel to each other, rude to their parents and unable to control their impulsive (read: stupid) urges, but instead haven't developed the gray matter to think of more acceptable forms of communication and behavior.

On the other hand, am I the only one who thinks this might be a bit of a cop out?

It seems brain research may turn out to be the perfect excuse when teens insult and exclude each other, or when they deface school property or respond disrespectfully to teachers and other adults.

As the findings of this research are applied, will a lack of brain maturity become the all-purpose excuse that permits bullying and vandalism? Will this discovery keep teens out of detention hall, or worse, prohibit school administrators from applying discipline to enforce standards of conduct?

Can't you just hear some high school senior's attorney arguing in court, "But Your Honor, my client *must* be permitted to graduate with his class. He simply has not developed the brain capacity to understand it is inappropriate to shout obscenities at his chemistry teacher while using a blowtorch to discover the combustive properties of nitroglycerin."

If you think this isn't coming, you don't read the paper much.

Neuroscience or not, I still think the age of reason comes at about seven. This is the age when I expect my children to understand that it's rude to be rude, it's unkind to be unkind, and it's dangerous to be dangerous.

I have to admit, however, that learning about the developing brain of teenagers does give me hope. (This is probably why the parents of young adults keep reassuring me that things get better).

In the meantime, I'm going to keep requiring that the teens around my house use what brain they have – or expect to answer that ridiculous question we parents can't help but ask.

Marybeth Hicks

Lesson one: Mom has feelings, too

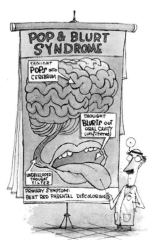

I s it any wonder women of a certain age sometimes experience a lack of self-confidence when our children ask questions such as, "Did you start bleaching your teeth? They don't look as yellow as they usually do."

Realizing the gaffe, the child attempts to salve your wounded feelings: "They weren't that yellow, really. I just noticed they look different. I mean, better."

Never mind that mom is embarrassed, self-conscious and concerned that her smile formerly resembled George Washington's.

I usually try to maintain a brave facade with my children when it comes to hurt feelings. I do this to model the wisdom of ignoring people who are insensitive.

Also, I do it because the whole process of becoming a mother leaves a woman with very little personal dignity, and I'm trying to preserve the meager portion I have left.

Stoicism aside, there comes a time when children need to know that moms have feelings, too.

Case in point: the day last fall when I had my hair done ("done" meaning cut, colored, styled and sprayed to the tune of $120). After two hours in the salon, I felt pampered and pretty.

I appeared freshly coifed at a high school cross-country meet where my two daughters would compete. Striding confidently to the area where the team was gathered, I waved to Betsy, then turned to see Katie in animated conversation with her fellow runners.

Just then Katie caught my eye, smiled and shouted her greeting for all to hear: "Hi, Mom. Did you get your hair colored? It looks darker."

It would have been hard to miss that my hair looked darker. When I consulted my stylist that morning, I lifted my long locks, pointed to the brownest shade on my head and said, "Let's make it all this color."

Still, I would have preferred if the adults with whom I stood could have done the socially appropriate thing and pretended they didn't notice the change.

Instead, Katie's comment prompted a full-blown symposium among the parents about hair color, including the relative merits of going gray, why men look distinguished and women look haggard as we age, and the going rate for highlights.

I've been a mom long enough to know that children simply must blurt out what pops into their heads. They don't yet have filters between the brain and the mouth to prohibit the odd question or comment whenever it occurs to them, even if the passing thought will compromise mom's delicate sense of propriety.

This is why women everywhere must suffer while standing at the grocery store checkout when a child looks up at her and says, "What's that big red thing on your chin?" (Or worse, "Eew, gross. There's something hanging from your nose.")

Dignity? Be serious.

I suppose it would be a genuinely self-possessed woman, if not an earthy one, who could respond, "It's a pimple, honey. Women get them when our hormones surge or when we're really stressed out. I spent 10 minutes this morning trying to hide it with concealer, but the makeup has worn off. I guess Mommy needs to touch it up, huh?"

I'm not that self-assured.

I respond like this: "Here's a quarter. Go get a gum ball." Then I prop my elbow on that little shelf meant for writing checks, sink my chin into my cupped hand and attempt to hide both the offending blemish and my embarrassment.

At some point – perhaps when one of my children conspicuously asked if I knew that my pants were too short – I realized I haven't done an adequate job of conveying to them that mothers are, in fact, people with feelings.

This is an eye-opener for most children. They think of us as "bionic moms" – flesh on the outside, mechanical on the inside – maternal machines whose only emotional concerns are for the well-being and happiness of our offspring.

Revealing our true emotional selves is critical. Otherwise, how can we teach them that everyone has feelings that can be injured and that kindness and charity begin at home? They need to know that mothers are first and foremost grown women who deserve thoughtfulness and respect.

Without this life lesson, we could end up with a generation of self-absorbed, insensitive buffoons; children who "dis" their moms and everyone else they encounter.

Oh wait. We have that.

Let's just say I'm doing my part to mitigate the cultural trend toward bluntness.

I don't recall the comment that caused me to snap, but finally I did. We were in the van – a great place to snap if you must because your children are captive – and I let loose with a list of offenses I have endured, or at least a few that illustrated my point.

I confess I exaggerated my emotional distress to encourage genuine remorse, but you could hardly blame me.

By the time I was finished, I had conducted a guided tour on a guilt trip intended to raise the collective consciousness of my brood. I think I even yelled something like, "Come hell or high water, I'm going to teach you how to be nice" (all the more effective with the veins popping out of my neck).

I can't say for sure if it worked, but the other day, I walked into the living room and one of my girls asked, "What's that smell?"

Lucky for her, she liked my cologne.

Marybeth Hicks

Dinner with SpongeBob

Ever since our two older girls stopped ordering off the children's menu, we don't go out to dinner much. They eat like linebackers, despite their angular adolescent figures, and one of them only likes steak. It gets expensive.

But this is the first day of a four-day weekend, and instead of letting them sleep in, I inflicted a day of hardship on my children by requiring them to help me clean the house. I even insisted they clean under the bathroom sink, and eliminate the mildew in the shower.

By late afternoon, even I am sick of the chores I invent. The kitchen is so clean, having been wiped down a couple of times, that I'm not willing to mess it up by cooking dinner, so I announce we are going out to eat.

What ensues is an all-family restaurant negotiation. There stand the six of us, coats on, ready to go, trying to agree on cuisine. Chinese? No. Pizza? We eat too much pizza. Mexican? The lines are too long. Italian? Too expensive. Every other suggestion is the neighborhood pub up the road by the shopping center. They have burgers and beer for the grown ups, a pretty good children's menu, and it's never crowded. Plus, it's not too pricey. We're agreed.

Now, I should mention it is Valentine's eve, and since my husband and I are going out the next night on our own, we bring little Valentine's gifts for the children. Each one gets a card and a book. This will be important later.

We get to the restaurant and, as usual, there are open tables, no waiting. I ask if we can sit near the fireplace but the waiter says it isn't working, so he seats us at the front of the room, a mere four feet from a television screen the size of Canada. And then, to be nice, he puts on *SpongeBob SquarePants*.

Don't get me wrong, I like SpongeBob. It's creative and cool, and even if the characters get naked, it doesn't matter because they're sea creatures. It's low risk, from a parenting perspective. The dining room has two additional TV monitors hanging on the walls, and those feature a celebrity basketball game in which child star Frankie Muniz is playing.

Well, needless to say, I cannot get the attention of my children in this room if my hair catches fire. Unless, while performing stop-drop-and roll, I were to block their view of SpongeBob.

My husband and I pique their interest briefly by handing out Valentine's gifts, but I mean briefly. Like three minutes. After that, their jaws slacken and return to Patrick's misadventures, or during a commercial, to Frankie's defensive skills.

The waiter manages to get them to articulate their dinner orders through the drool that hangs off their open lips.

This seems pathetic to me, so I point out that watching TV isn't very social. When the food comes and they're still glazed over, I ask the waiter to turn off Spongebob.

What I mean is, actually cut the power to the larger than life images dancing behind my head. Instead, he changes the channel on the big screen to the celebrity basketball game. God forbid we eat without entertainment.

But I am not deterred. I want family fun. Friday night karaoke is about to begin and I ask for the song menu. The waiter seems surprised, which offends me a little. (Just because I don't want my kids to watch Spongebob while they eat doesn't mean I'm not fun. Whatever.)

I peruse the list but right away, Katie (a high school freshman) is resisting. No, she won't sing a Dixie Chicks song. Not even with her sister. Certainly not with me.

I put her name on a slip of paper anyway and send it to the karaoke guy, but when he calls out the song, she won't go up and instead gets huffy.

Betsy and I decide to sing Patsy Cline's *Crazy* – the most popular karaoke song in America. So we're not original. We think we can hit the high notes.

While we're up there trashing this country classic, I look over at my table to find the high schooler reading her new book, as opposed to slashing her wrists with a butter knife, and everyone else – including my husband – looking away with expressions that say, "I don't know those two. If we leave at the same time, it's just a coincidence."

When we do leave, I feel dopey for working so hard to create family fun. I know you're supposed to let family evenings unfold as they will and not expect everyone to have the script that's available only to the cast of *The Cosby Show.*

I'm wishing I remembered that the mom of a high schooler should try to impersonate a potted plant to the degree she is able.

And I realize that after a long day of chores, all they really want to do is eat and watch Spongebob. Together. As a family.

Marybeth Hicks

Social life?
What social
life?

Let this be an open apology to all the couples I once judged as socially inattentive – not that you knew I felt this way.

In fact, let this be my confession that I secretly thought you were inappropriately consumed with the interests and extracurricular activities of your children.

Chalk it up to lack of experience, naivety about the way parenting really works in our day and age. Let's just say I didn't know what I didn't know.

And you, well, you were too busy chaperoning the school dance and shopping for snacks for the soccer team to notice that I thought you were neglectful.

At the time, my children were still small – two were as yet unborn – and life was simple. They had no curricula, much less a schedule of extracurricular activities. A busy day included an hour of *Sesame Street,* an afternoon at the kitchen table with Play-Doh and cookie cutters, a walk, a snack, a nap and a bath. By 7:30 each night, they were tucked into bed, and I was emancipated.

Back then, I spent my spare time finding ways to interact with adults. I formed a book club, and I actually read the books before the club met.

I joined volunteer groups and attended lots of meetings – because bettering my community also enabled me to gather with other women who were unlikely to spill juice on me.

In addition to stretching my literary consumption and my community service muscle, I entertained – and I used actual china, not Chinet.

My husband and I regularly hosted other couples for dinner parties, and our friends reciprocated. We went with friends to movies, sporting events and even occasionally to a play or a concert.

Soon enough, however, I noticed a change in our social circle. We would get together at the home of friends only to discover that a few couples had begged off the invitation because of conflicts in their schedules – conflicts such as dance recitals and soccer tournaments.

The friends whose children were Cub Scouts or Brownies called only when it was time to sell popcorn or cookies.

The friends whose boys played in the youth hockey league dropped off the face of the earth.

I sanctimoniously vowed my family wouldn't fall into the trap of child-centered insanity. I had grown up just fine without spending my afternoons bouncing from one activity to the next, and I decided my children could do the same.

That just goes to show how much I didn't know.

My downfall came when I thought I could limit my children to the offerings in the local parks and recreation catalog. I rationalized that I would ferry them only as far as the community center for tap lessons that met just once a week for eight weeks – not that you could learn any real tap-dancing in that short span, but at least it wasn't overly intrusive on our time.

Then, in the time it takes to say, "How many days a week do we practice?" my life took a turn, and it's never been the same.

Introductory dance classes became 12 weekends a year on the road to dance competitions. Instructional basketball evolved into a travel team that plays on weekends in the summer. A minor role in a school play became a six-week drama camp with evening rehearsals and two performances.

To be more involved in the lives of our children, my husband became the basketball coach. To supervise their activities appropriately, I became the volunteer coordinator for the school play.

Multiply our commitments times four (because it wouldn't be fair to coach one child and not our other three), and what you get is a former social life and friends to whom you say things like, "We should get together sometime."

Sigh.

We became the kind of couple I looked down on a dozen years ago for living vicariously through their children.

But as I said, back when my family was young, I didn't know what I didn't know.

For example, I didn't know how invested I would be in watching my son on a basketball court, putting his all into the game, learning tenacity and teamwork. I didn't know how important it would be to him that I come to all his games and cheer him on.

I didn't know how much my daughters would be able to learn from running, dance, music and drama beyond the ability to compete and perform. I didn't realize that the poise they could gain in those settings would help them be more confident in life. And I didn't know how crucial it would be to stand at the finish line or sit in the audience just to offer moral support.

I also didn't anticipate the new friendships that would occupy this season of my life – I didn't know how close I would grow with the parents whose schedules mirror mine and whose parenting journeys I share with such enthusiasm.

It has been a long time since I misjudged those couples who disappeared from our social life into the lives of their children. One of these days, when I'm finished doing the same, I plan to look them up and have them over for dinner.

Which reminds me, I wonder where I put the china?

Marybeth Hicks

Tooth Fairy isn't perfect – neither is mom

Of all the roles associated with parenthood – valet, chauffeur, personal chef, personal trainer, appointment secretary, private tutor, long-range planner, financial adviser and psychoanalyst – the one at which I am an abject failure is Tooth Fairy.

Listen, I am just as excited as the next parent when my children go through phases of growth and development, and this includes the fun of seeing them lose their teeth, offering months of gummy grins and charming lisps

Toothless children are cute, especially when they try to pronounce Saskatchewan or eat corn on the cob or blow bubble gum into huge orbs through the temporary gaps in their mouths.

As a function of parenting, however, the whole Tooth Fairy thing eluded me from the beginning. You might think I'm exaggerating, but I'm not.

Here is what happened the first time my eldest daughter lost a tooth: Bedtime came, not early enough for once, and with it the rituals of bathing, brushing and prayers. I tucked 7-year-old Katie into bed and listened to her ask God to bless "our whole family and especially the Tooth Fairy, that she has a safe journey to the space under my pillow."

Naturally, given her excitement, sleep came reluctantly. I checked on her a few times in an effort to accomplish the fairylike duties that were my maternal obligation, but she wasn't giving up easily. She wanted to see the Tooth Fairy – meet her in person – maybe play together for a while in the soft glow of the streetlights streaming through her windows.

Eventually I forgot why I was waiting and went to bed.

The next morning, Katie came rushing down the hallway and burst into our bedroom. "Guess what the Tooth Fairy left under my pillow? My tooth." Then came the sobbing and self-pity. ("It's my first tooth, and the Tooth Fairy didn't even care.")

My heart sank.

I intended to be the perfect mom by rewarding her bravery in the face of this dental rite of passage, and instead I blew my debut appearance as the Tooth Fairy.

I feigned confusion, said something like, "There must be an explanation," and shot my husband a look that meant "cover for me." Racing downstairs, I dashed off a note with my left hand (a clever disguise of handwriting), slipped it into an envelope along with a dollar bill and taped it to the window at the front door.

The note said: "I cannot get into your house unless you leave the front door unlocked. Here is your money. Please leave the tooth under your pillow again tonight. I will pick it up. Don't forget to leave the door open. T.F."

It was a lame attempt to cover my ineptitude, but she bought it.

Subsequent efforts to maintain the Tooth Fairy fantasy have met with similar results, but I've learned to accept that this is one area of parenting at which I'm inconsistent, at best. Sometimes the fairy shows up; sometimes she doesn't.

More often than not, when the children in my home lose a tooth, they hand over the ivory and collect the cash, recognizing that an imperfect Tooth Fairy is still a source of income. Thankfully, my children no longer take personally the fairy's slights; I think they finally understand she's doing the best she can.

As with many aspects of parenting, I never appreciated the lengths the Tooth Fairy takes to fulfill her duties until I became a Tooth Fairy myself.

I know I'll never be perfect, but I still have one child left challenging me to improve. Now the 7-year-old is Amy, who constantly wiggles and wonders when the next tooth will fall out, making way for permanent – though grossly crooked – choppers.

On a recent visit with my parents, just before I tucked her into bed, Amy lost her fourth tooth, a tiny white reminder of the baby who once cried for days when it cut through her gums to create her endearing smile.

As usual, we put the tooth in a baggie and slid it under her pillow. Then I closed the bedroom door and promptly erased my Tooth Fairy role from my mind. I mean, I literally never gave it another thought – a fatally flawed fairy, that's me.

In the morning, Amy waited for her grandparents to awaken and announced to them, "Guess what the Tooth Fairy left under my pillow? My tooth." Shades of her sister.

"I even left her a note," my daughter explained. "A friend of mine left a note asking the Tooth Fairy for 20 dollars, and she got it. So I left a note and asked for 50." Precocious? Perhaps. Obnoxious? Obviously.

Her grandfather (aka "Puppa"), moved by her resourcefulness, if not her business acumen, sneaked possession of the baggie and her note to the Tooth Fairy. He removed the tooth, slipped her reward inside and dashed off a reply: "This is only a 20-dollar tooth."

It occurred to me she might have figured out the whole Tooth Fairy thing, what with the fairy's delayed appearance. "Did someone tell you I'm the Tooth Fairy?" asked her later that day.

She looked at me a bit incredulously. "You're not the Tooth Fairy, Mom. Puppa is."

She got that right. There's no way I would give her 20 bucks for a tooth.

Marybeth Hicks

This is not a threat, it's a promise

I t was only the first hole, but already the bickering on the mini golf course was intense. My son, exhibiting the hypercompetitive nature that wins games but annoys other people, took on the responsibility to coach his younger sister on her putting technique.

"That's not how you do it," he said impatiently.

"I can do it any way I want," she argued.

"You're doing it wrong," he said.

"Who made you the golf police?" she countered.

This exchange was going nowhere, not to mention they both held putters in hand, ready to employ as weapons at any moment. "Enough," I shouted. "If I hear one more fight between the two of you, you're toast."

What it means to be "toast" isn't entirely clear, but they eased up a bit. They know me well enough to assume I'll come up with some miserable consequence, like sending them ahead to play the last few holes together – alone – where the rest of the family doesn't have to hear them fight. "Toast" is vague enough to keep me from having to act, which makes it an all-purpose worst outcome.

The problem with making threats to children while in a fit of parental frustration is that you have to remember what you said you'd do, and then later, when your children don't live up to your standards of behavior, you have to follow through and do it.

I've learned a lot about making threats in my 15 years as a parent. First, I've learned that there are just two kinds of threats – the kind you'll never carry out and the kind you must. For example, when I find mountains of shoes piled on the landing by the back door instead of stored in the baskets where they belong, I threaten to burn all the shoes in our possession and force my children into a barefoot existence.

When they leave toys all over the house, I say I'm going to donate their stuff to charity and force them to play with lint from the dryer.

When they waste food, I threaten to serve cereal for every meal.

They don't really expect to be shoeless, toyless cereal eaters. What they expect instead is to endure a lengthy lecture laced with horrible punishments that sound unenforceable and unlikely.

On the other hand, I also have learned there are some threats you absolutely must make good on or risk losing any semblance of parental authority. These are the kind I really hate because, invariably, following through is more difficult for me than for my children.

Case in point: the girls' bedroom. My two older daughters – both teens – share a room that resembles a landfill. The clothes we spend hours choosing at the mall become wrinkled balls of fabric in the corners. Those would be the clean clothes. Inexplicably, the dirty clothes often are hung – askew – on hangers in the closet.

Towels are single-use items, stored after each shower in wet piles where they ferment into mildewed stench bombs.

Their bathroom sink stores everything they need to be beautiful: hairbrushes, makeup, razors, dental floss (used), blobs of toothpaste, tops of empty shampoo bottles, bowls from yesterday's ice cream, someone's English homework, a hammer (a hammer?).

Not long ago, on a rare visit to this condemned corner of our abode, I took a stand. "Let's get one thing straight: This is not your house. This house belongs to Dad and me, and you only live here out of our benevolent generosity. When you own a house, you may choose to live like slobs, but as long as you live under our roof ... blah, blah, blah." If you're a parent, you can fill in the rest.

In the midst of my tirade, I made a new threat. I said they had the remainder of the school year to prove they understood the house rules about clean bedrooms. If I didn't see an improvement, I'd switch their room with their younger sister's – a much smaller space not really suited for two teenage girls.

"It would be cramped and cluttered, but at least I'd have a smaller mess to endure when I walk past your door."

I don't really want to spend a weekend moving furniture, nor do I want to force my younger daughter to relinquish the only pink space in the house.

Every time I stick my head into the teenagers' room and see an unmade bed or a pile of clean laundry that didn't make it into a dresser, I wish I hadn't threatened the bedroom switch because it looks as if I'm going to have to actually do it. Worse yet, changing rooms probably won't cause my teens to adopt an organized lifestyle anyway.

Fortunately, at the end of my monologue on housekeeping, I remembered to throw in this little maternal gem: "And another thing – I reserve the right to change this punishment at any time if I decide some other consequence would be more effective – like moving you both to the garage."

It's the threat they know I won't fulfill – the empty promise – that gives them another chance to improve their behavior.

Then again, one night in the garage can't hurt them. I could throw some sleeping bags out there between the van and the bicycles and tuck them in with a reminder not to trip over the basketballs if they come in during the night to use the bathroom.

Lucky for my girls, the last time I visited their bedroom, it was spotless.

Marybeth Hicks

Family fits together like pieces of a puzzle

T he clearance price attracts my attention first. Next is the idyllic scene on the cover of the box – two Adirondack chairs angled gracefully on the front porch of a lovely clapboard house; a cat perched on the front stoop; a dogwood tree in full bloom in the yard.

The only thing missing in the photo is me, sitting in one of those worn wooden chairs, sipping iced tea and reading the newest copy of *O: The Oprah Magazine* or a book of poems by Billy Collins.

I pick up the box and study the photo, deciding I easily could spend a weekend dreaming about a place as quiet and quaint as this. Besides, the pharmacy put the puzzles on deep discount, probably to make room for beach chairs and water wings. At $2.99, reconstructing the thousand pieces in this box is cheap entertainment.

My husband says there are people who do puzzles and people who don't. He doesn't. It's not a question of whether he enjoys the process, it's that he doesn't "think spatially." I'm not surprised when he surveys the cardboard cutouts on the coffee table and decrees, "This is not how people have fun."

"You're missing out," I say cheerfully. But Jim declares the puzzle "impossible." I'm not deterred. It's a long weekend, we have no plans, snow is flying outside, and I have a fire roaring at my back – not to mention, the puzzle is not the point.

As soon as I get started, two of my children scurry across the room and stake out spots on the floor beside me. We sort out the edge pieces and begin assembling the frame. Every coupling elicits a victory whisper. Within an hour, the 20-by-24-inch border claims its space in the center of the table, leaving little room for the roughly 930 puzzle pieces remaining.

We find all the red, white and blue pieces that will depict "Old Glory" hanging off the front of a white pillar. Now we realize roughly 600 pieces of this puzzle are white – parts of the six pillars graciously holding up the roof of my imaginary retreat. Intimidated, we move on to the cobblestone steps at the bottom of the frame.

Every so often, there's a staff change among my puzzle helpers. One quits for a while to rest her eyes, another takes a break for popcorn. Replacements take over (but not Jim) – or sometimes, I just work on the puzzle by myself, offering an unspoken invitation to join me to anyone who walks through the room.

Basketball is on TV, then the news, then *Law and Order*. One by one, I kiss and tuck the children away for the night – by the time I turn the lights out on the puzzle, it's going on one in the morning

Piece by piece, the weekend progresses. Hostas take form in the lower right corner; the dark, blurry pieces we thought were the front door turn out to be a window. The pillars aren't just white, but varying shades of white. We study the photo on the box, passing it around in hopes it will reveal the key to making the hundreds of remaining puzzle pieces fit together easily, – without testing, turning, trying.

What I learn while puzzling is not about the puzzle, but about the puzzlers. Heads nearly touching while we study the rainbow of blacks that eventually will be the screen door; I ask about school or sports or social plans; they share thoughts about teachers and friends.

Jimmy tells me how he'll miss the boy in his class visiting from South Korea.

Amy tells me what she loves about the movie *Napoleon Dynamite*.

Betsy talks about enrolling for high school and choosing her classes for next year.

Katie tells me about the book she's reading and why it's both interesting and disturbing.

Gradually, as the picture on the coffee table reflects more and more the cover of the puzzle box, my family invests itself not only in the shared challenge of an "impossible" task, but also in conversation about a host of topics from the TV show *The Apprentice* to our dinner plans to what we love about summer.

Eventually, even my non-puzzling husband joins us, inspired by my tenacity – or is it my relentless dedication, despite the meaninglessness of its purpose? More likely, it's starting to look like fun.

Jim's puzzling technique is methodical, if not brooding. He doesn't pick up pieces and try them – he waits until he sees the exact puzzle piece for a specific place and then confidently drops it there. It's slow, but successful.

Two days into the puzzle project, we're amazed at what we're accomplishing. My son lobbies to extract a promise from me that he will be the one to insert the final piece. It's premature to argue over this honor – there are easily 100 pieces left, all indistinguishable shades of olive green. "Whoever has the last piece will put it in the puzzle," I say.

The six of us hover over the coffee table as we work furiously toward the finish. Just 12 pieces left; now nine; now five. Suddenly, it looks as if we've lost one, which prompts us to scour the floor. Someone suggests maybe the dog ate it.

Then, silently, Jim takes my hand and slides the missing piece into my palm. I smile at him as I slip it into place, completing a serene picture that was neither impossible nor even very puzzling after all.

Marybeth Hicks

Raspberries in Mom's face? Whatever

whatever....

T he line at the electronics superstore winds from the service desk to the front doors. Apparently, I'm not the only person who noticed the 30-day warranties on our broken holiday gift gadgets are about to expire.

I amble into the queue, holding tight to the bag containing a nonfunctioning wireless mouse and an uncooperative Dance Dance Revolution game (my daughter's, not mine).

My thoughts drift to the evening's dinner plan. Staring at the speckled linoleum floor, I imagine ways to cook chicken breast without cream of mushroom soup. My thoughts are disrupted when a little boy wanders away from the line behind me and his mom says, "Ben, come back here. Someone might take you."

From the corner of my eye, I see Ben smile at her and take another step away from his mother.

I can't say I blame him. He's only about 4, but even he knows her warning is extreme. It's unlikely he'll be snatched from the superstore while standing eight feet from his mother. He's checking her credibility.

"Benny, I mean it," his mom says. "Do you want someone to take you? Come and stand next to me."

Maybe he does want someone to take him. I turn to watch Benny's response. His eyes shift from his mom to me. He grins. He giggles. Then he gives his mother a huge, wet "raspberry." Slobber sprays off his face onto the floor.

"Benjamin," his mother reprimands. "Do you see this long line? If you wander into the store I'll have to come and get you, and that means I'll lose my place and we'll have to go to the back of the line. Do you want to go to the back of the line and start waiting all over again?"

That's ridiculous because Benjamin isn't waiting in line as it is. I give her credit for logic, but she's dealing with a 4-year-old, so it's wasted. Besides, it's clear to both Benny and me that she's more concerned about keeping her place in line than getting her child to obey her command.

Benjamin does just what you would expect from a boy who has heard his share of idle threats. He takes two more steps backward, sticks his tongue between his lips and sprays his mother again, this time bigger, louder and wetter than before, his eyes glowing with a demonic twinkle.

Did I mention the line is long? The tug of war between Benny Boy and his mom continues endlessly while we inch forward. I resist the urge to help this woman by snapping at her son, "Listen up, Ben. Get in line now before you and your mother make me criminally insane."

Benjamin's mom heaves a heavy sigh into the back of my jacket. I remember what it's like to have a defiant preschooler, and I sense her frustration, but what's really running through my mind is, "Lady, you're toast. You think little Benny is tough now? Just wait until he's 15."

Lest I seem unsympathetic, let me just say, I'm unsympathetic. This is because I once was the mom in the superstore whose child tested the limits and bolted from the line. But somewhere in the back of my parent psyche was a tiny voice counseling me, "Never negotiate with a 4-year-old."

Ben is testing his mother's authority, and that's his job. This is how 4-year-olds find their limits. Mom's job is to set those limits and stick to them.

I do deep-breathing exercises, trying to ignore their annoying battle of wills. Only my proximity to the front of the line keeps me from turning around and saying, "If you want little Benny to cooperate, you need to follow through. If he were my kid, I'd be out in the parking lot having a nose-to-nose chat with Ben to let him know my expectations for this shopping trip. Then I'd come back inside, go to the end of the line like I promised, and chat with my son while we waited. If he wandered off again, we'd start all over until we got it right. It's time-consuming, inconvenient – even exasperating – but do you want a child who obeys you or not?"

It's a great speech, but I don't give it.

Instead, when the sales associate says, "I can help the next person in line," I dart toward the service desk and do my business, thankful that Benny's mom is called to the opposite end of the counter.

From my brief observation, Ben's mother looks like one of those parents who applies reason and hopes her child eventually will respond respectfully to her requests.

I don't think her strategy is going to work.

Today's raspberry in mom's face is tomorrow's "Whatever," spoken with teenage disdain when Ben walks out the door with the car keys and his mom shouts, "Be home before 11."

One of these days, when he's slamming doors in her face, yelling about her rules and ignoring her repeated warnings, she may wonder how Ben turned into such an unruly teenager. She probably won't see a connection to episodes like the one in the superstore when her son was just a child.

Benny's mom got a refund for her unwanted item, but she bought herself a couple of raspberries instead, and those are nonreturnable.

Marybeth Hicks

No point arguing when Mom's answer is 'no'

You can't wear those shorts to church," I said to my teenage daughter. It was a simple statement – an efficient act of parenting, combining an observation and a directive in one quick but unmistakable declarative sentence.

Right away, she argued with me. "Everyone wears shorts to church in the summer."

She has a point. Living in a college town means the attire at our church falls somewhere between "Sunday best" and "vintage vagabond." Disheveled often is the best some parishioners can do. I try not to pass judgment on the clothing choices people make for weekly worship and instead focus on the fact that the place fills each week with college students who take some time out for God.

Still, my understanding attitude about church attire doesn't extend to my own children. We have standards – minimal though they are – and the "Daisy Duke" shorts my daughter selected this morning aren't appropriate.

Her argument is pointless, though I love her line of reasoning because it's so easy to unravel. "You're not everyone. Go change."

"I have nothing else to wear," she says. She must have forgotten I am the woman who purchases, washes and irons all of her clothes. I name a few alternatives and heap on the pressure to move quickly so as not to make the rest of us late.

I've read lots of advice about how to get children to cooperate. Experts say it's best to avoid "authoritarian" parenting and instead give children a range of acceptable choices so they can take ownership of decisions and feel empowered, responsible and proud. In theory, when they feel they're in control of a decision, children will respond willingly.

Avoiding authoritarianism certainly sounds nice, but I don't think it works. This is because my children would argue about what constitutes an acceptable choice and we would be back to square one.

Instead of responding favorably to a choice-driven parental directive such as, "You may choose a snack from either the fruit or vegetable drawer in the refrigerator," they would say this: "Why can't I have ice cream?" Next thing I know, I'm engaged in a debate about why ice cream is not a healthy choice, why I don't buy better ice cream flavors, and why a fruit-flavored Popsicle should be an alternative.

After about 15 minutes, I would hear, "I'm not hungry anyway," and that would be the end of it.

Instead of wasting a lot of time pretending I'm not making decisions, I just decide. "Have a banana" is so much more efficient than negotiating about the merits of fruit versus tutti-frutti.

Yet, because children are determined, if not relentless, my authoritarian style meets with the odd argument – "odd" here being a word that means constant and predictable.

Despite my consistency (also strongly recommended in the parenting literature), there is hardly a decision I make around my house that isn't met with debate. My children don't really expect me to change my mind, but they're optimists. They figure there's always the chance they'll catch me at a weak moment. What unbending creature would stick to her guns on everything?

Of course, they're right. If they hound, badger, nag and argue enough, I can't help but wear down like the tread of a new tire, softening against the rough, relentless road.

As with a tire, though, there's also a chance I'll blow up, which happens every so often when one child too many has heard my final answer yet submitted an appeal.

When this happens, I re-establish my parental primacy, and my vocabulary reacquaints itself with that one little word that gives parents the power to lead: no.

Television on a sunny summer afternoon? No.

Popcorn before dinner? No.

Rap on my car radio? No.

"Daisy Duke" shorts to church on Sunday? No, no, a thousand times no.

My answers are non-negotiable, my tone of voice convincing, my resolve apparent. It works for any issue that needs resolution, from choosing whose turn it is to "ride shotgun" in the van to deciding which child will empty the dishwasher, which one will reload it, and who will escape kitchen duty for no good reason.

When it's clear I'm back on track and their persistent arguments are pointless, something strange and wonderful revisits my home: order. I speaketh, and it is done.

Not to mention, knowing I mean business on minor matters sends a strong and useful message about the big ones.

I'm sure my children would like to make more decisions about what they eat and wear and do with their leisure time, but I'm not worried that my authoritarian parenting style will rob them of an ability to make choices. I'm not eager to rear a bunch of indecisive, dependent, opinionless people, and anyway, they get plenty of chances to commandeer their destinies.

Then again, because they're growing up in a house where their parents make a fair number of rules and expect compliance, I hope our influence wears off on them.

Long after they free themselves from my authoritarian clutches, when at last they're the ones choosing the snacks and determining their schedules and outfitting themselves each day, I have high hopes that their lost arguments will result in good decisions.

Maybe they'll occasionally choose to eat carrot sticks, after which they'll put themselves to bed before midnight and, the next day, wear something respectful if the occasion calls for it.

You can't argue; that would be good.

Marybeth Hicks

Emergency room is filled with experts

The muffled sound of *Pop Goes the Weasel* being played on the piano comes from the basement. Down the hall, the computer printer rhythmically churns out a document. The washing machine and dryer quietly hum from the laundry room, while construction crews outside my open windows send echoes through the autumn afternoon as they piece together the home that will house my new neighbors.

All of it combines to create a melodic soundtrack for my life. Then, amid the jingling of my dog's tags as he wanders from room to room, and the voice of SpongeBob from behind a door (where someone thinks I don't know she's watching television), there is the now familiar hacking cough that plagues my eldest daughter.

It started with a head cold two weeks ago. Then, because she suffers from asthma, it sank to her chest and became a persistent cough. With the geese overhead honking at one another, it's hard to tell whether she's clearing her airways or flying south for the winter.

Finally, last Tuesday, with Katie writhing on the living room floor trying to reach for the bottom of her lungs with every breath – sounding for all the world like a tuba tuning up for a concert – I dialed our pediatrician's home number. It pays to be friends with your pediatrician.

I didn't have to convince him it was serious. He could barely hear me over the phone since her uncontrollable coughing drowned out our conversation. "I think you'd better take her to the emergency room," said my friend the doctor.

It's the phrase every mother knows is coming but hates to hear. A trip to the emergency room on a Tuesday evening at 10:00 will not end until 2:00 a.m. the next day, at best – and that's if a coughing fit buys us a seat at the front of the triage line.

We climb into the van and head downtown to the hospital. She's still hacking as we walk past a group of teens gathered at the ambulance entrance, where one of them is wearing a hospital bracelet but wandering around in an agitated state. From somewhere in the darkness, a mother's voice says, "That's enough. Settle down."

We sign in. We sit down. We wait. Across the room are two girls with injuries sustained playing basketball – one holds a bloody towel on her ragged lower lip, the other has ice on her swollen knee. Their mothers sit close, adjusting bandages and speaking in low, reassuring tones.

My daughter and I sit next to a young mom whose child naps on her lap. We strike up a friendly chat but our words are punctuated by Katie's relentless cough. I rub her back and try to help her calm her breathing.

Finally, the nurse calls and we move to the receiving room for an initial interview. After taking my daughter's temperature, blood pressure and weight, the usual drill, the nurse moves us directly to an exam room, confirming that Katie is in bad shape.

The visit to the ER unfolds as they always do, but after 16 years of motherhood and four children, I'm not afraid the way I was when they were small. Besides, it's always easier when the patient can respond intelligently. It used to be my children kept me guessing between a miserable cry, a whiney cry or a desperate cry.

There are doctors and nurses in and out of our cube. The resident suggests we prepare for the possibility that Katie will be admitted, but soon enough the attending physician visits and lets us know we'll be heading home before the sun comes up.

They give Katie something to calm her cough and help her to fall asleep, and then the inevitable waiting begins as we see how she responds. Sure enough, she drifts off into a drug-induced nap while I stroke her hair and watch her eyelids flutter.

Sitting by her side, behind the curtain that pretends to offer privacy, I listen to the quiet conversations of the experts beyond the veil. Their depth of knowledge amazes me as they assess the patients in their care and offer suggestions based on years of hard-won experience

It's not the doctors I'm hearing, but the mothers. Hovering over hospital gurneys, they advocate for a daughter here, a son over there, providing history and context and expected results for the children whose fragile health they work to improve.

My daughter takes a deep, cleansing breath and I wait for the heavy sound of the cough that inevitably will follow, but it doesn't come. Instead, she rolls gently under the flannel hospital blanket and sinks deeper into sleep. I ease back in my chair and close my eyes.

I remember all the nights I've spent walking hospital hallways with a baby in my arms or soothing a toddler into sitting still for an x-ray or holding down a child for stitches or the sharp point of a needle.

My memories become dreams and then I catch my head nodding forward. Time to wake up. In a few minutes, the nurse will return with discharge orders and I'll be driving the empty city streets back home.

When we climb in the van my groggy daughter whispers, "I love you, Mom," and then drifts back to sleep. It's just another night in the ER, but then again, there's no place else I'd rather be.

Marybeth Hicks

Love of a dad defies all logic

'**W**here is the damn battery?" My husband's voice carries through the hallway from the den to the kitchen, conveying his irritation in every precisely articulated syllable.

I jump into situations such as this to defuse his frustration. While he pulls cushions off the chairs to find the missing AA battery that powers the remote control, I act as a sounding board for his – let's say, reflections – on parenthood.

What should be a simple task of finding and replacing a battery often turns into a running commentary on important concerns, such as why the piece that encloses the batteries is missing from the remote control in the first place.

While he's mulling that over, Jim wonders who left the lights on in the empty basement, how the dog escaped into the neighborhood without a leash or someone to walk him, and who left a half glass of milk on the kitchen counter to spoil.

There's only one answer, of course: the children

"If you wanted to go through life without a broken remote control, you should not have married me and had four kids," I remind him.

"That's ridiculous," he grumbles.

That children break things and lose stuff confounds my otherwise rational husband. For reasons I can't conceive, he thinks it is entirely plausible and even expected that his offspring should maneuver their bikes in and out of the garage without bumping into our cars, for example.

He seems surprised if someone shatters a dish into tiny shards or backs up a toilet by using too much tissue or writes with permanent marker on a piece of wood furniture or misplaces a pair of shoes.

Of course, this is because he's approaching the issue from the wrong point of view. You can't look at your children with a rational eye, expecting reason and logic in their behavior.

They are people who think a fat guy in a red suit can fit down a chimney and bring them toys, for heaven's sake. There is nothing logical about them.

The only way to maintain sanity in parenthood is to suspend all rational thought and recognize that a day without a costly mishap is just lucky.

Of all the things about fatherhood for which Jim was unprepared, the hidden costs are highest on the list. He didn't anticipate the reams of paper that would end up as pictures on our refrigerator, the gallons of water that would run down our driveway and into the street on summer afternoons or the juice that would trickle down the drain after a child took only a sip from a full glass.

He didn't know about the high cost of hair accessories, the fees for late rental movies and lost library books, or the added tips he would leave to compensate over-worked busboys charged with cleaning up our restaurant messes.

Despite nearly 17 years in the parenting trenches, Jim still clings to the notion that most of our hidden expenses could be avoided if our children would only (fill in logical behavior here).

On the other hand, my husband is a savvy consumer. He's not one to make an investment without making sure he receives an adequate return. In his logical mind, if there are hidden costs to fatherhood, there also had better be hidden benefits.

Fortunately, for every broken basketball net, there are hours on the driveway playing games of one-on-one with a son who idolizes him.

For every dollar spent repairing a musical instrument, there's a virtuoso perfor-mance just for Dad in the kitchen by an adoring daughter.

For all the mishaps that wind up in broken lamps and cracked picture frames, there's the sound of exuberant laughter right before the inevitable thud.

For all the days filled with the stress of providing for a family that seems deter-mined to stretch his resources to their limits, there are bedtimes with tender conver-sations and prayers recited softly in the shadows.

Defying all logic, fatherhood holds this sweet, unexpected irony: The more it costs you, the richer you are.

The trick, of course, is to remember this while you are hunting down the lost bat-tery for the broken remote control or taking a cold shower thanks to teenagers who use all the hot water in the tank.

Fortunately, children have a knack for putting life into its proper perspective, and in our house, it doesn't take much to transform Dad from riled and rational to forgiv-ing and fun. Probably this is because Jim is not about to waste the time and treasure he has put into building our family.

Loving our children beyond reason means accepting that his life is defined not by his personal achievements or the creature comforts he provides us, but by the sacrifices it takes to be a father.

Where's the logic in that?

I guess it only goes to show that men aren't always the rational people they pro-fess to be.

Then again, I suspect Jim has done the math and he knows his payoff is waiting down the road. Dollar for dollar, his day-to-day investments in our children are his surest route to a lifetime of riches.

Marybeth Hicks

Family life is high finance

Most people have a system for handling the family finances. Some people use "tickler" files to remind them when the bills are due. Others use online bill-paying services, the newest trend in electronic banking.

My system is different. I know it's time to pay the bills when my back goes out.

I'm not kidding. My back muscles monitor the calendar and gradually tense up from around the 10th of each month (the day the mortgage payment is deducted automatically from our checking account and sent electronically to the bank) through the 26th, the closing date on our cell-phone account.

If I haven't set aside the time to organize the invoices, record the hundreds of debit-card receipts that fill the inside pocket of my purse, balance the checking account and pay the bills, the soft tissue surrounding my lower lumbar region seizes into a taut, tight muscular vise, gripping the adjacent nerves to send the "pain" message to my brain.

I'm even known for this. Not long ago, I stopped to see my sister. I gingerly stepped out of my van and slowly raised my torso to an upright position as she walked across her driveway to greet me.

"Ouch. Time to pay the bills, huh?" she said.

The good news is, I know exactly how to deal with this particular malady, but who would have figured the cure for back pain is monthly solvency?

Thus, I find myself sitting at my desk, calculator at the ready, embarking on the only task I can think of that is more painful than my wretched back spasms, but I can put if off no longer.

This month, the reason I want to avoid this task can be summed up in one word: orthodontia.

All four of our children – including our 8-year-old – require orthodontia, now in various stages. We have two in retainers, one in the "train track" phase and one whose future problems were so glaring we had to start her with palate expanders (essentially a "rack" designed to increase the size of the mouth while forcing moms and dads into the role of sadistic torturers).

Here's a factor one should consider when seeking out a life partner with whom to create a family: What is my potential mate's contribution to our dental gene pool?

I didn't consider this – I just went ahead and fell in love with a guy whose acute underbite I overlooked because it gives him a strong, masculine chin.

Admittedly, he didn't exactly get a fair shot at making an assessment of my impact on the teeth of our offspring. I had braces for three years as a girl, so all evidence of overcrowding was eliminated. My smile deceived.

Oh well. We probably would have married each other anyway on the assumption that crooked teeth skip a generation. I fill out check number six-gazillion-and-three, made payable to our orthodontist, tearing out the pay stubs from two payment books similar to the kind you get when you buy a house or a car.

Next, the stack of unavoidable household bills: garbage collection, water, electricity, cable service, pest control. (I tried to cut the pest guy from my budget once but discovered the mice in my neighborhood share information with each other about which houses are safe and which are not.)

Now to pay the insurance bills: auto, home, my husband's life, my life. Every time I write the check for my life insurance, I remind myself to show Jim my bookkeeping system in case he ever is forced to do this job. (Come to think of it, he would rather die first than do this job.)

With each check, I enter a "payee" and "amount" into my computerized check registry, which makes the sound of a cash register when I hit Enter. Cha-ching. Clearly, this was someone's idea of a cruel joke – someone who is young and unmarried and rich and works in Silicon Valley. Someone who probably doesn't have to deal with the mundane task of paying for a refrigerator repair.

The superfluous water dispenser on the front of the unit broke, leaking 14 gallons of water into the kitchen until the valve to the water line was discovered.

I have just written a check for the refrigerator repair when my daughter comes in and asks for money to buy school supplies.

This is not a good moment to ask me for so much as a stick of gum.

"You do realize money doesn't grow on trees?" I say irrelevantly.

Immediately I feel bad because it's not her fault the fridge broke or that she is required to go to school with an assortment of materials in her backpack. Besides, she knows money doesn't grow on trees; it comes from money machines.

After a lifetime of watching mom and dad drive up to a big box outside the bank, insert a plastic card and drive away with a walletful of greenbacks, children understandably are unaware that money doesn't just spew from cash machines on street corners the world over.

Once, one of my children asked if we could do something (Go out for ice cream? Buy a convertible? I forget.) and I said we didn't have the money. "Go to an ATM and get some," she said. "There's always money in the machine."

Would that this were true.

At last, the pile of bills is gone – for this month, at least. There's not much left in the checkbook, but then again, at least my back doesn't hurt.

Marybeth Hicks

Mother's Day isn't just the second Sunday in May

He meant well, but 15 years ago, my husband was young and inexperienced and unaware of the significance of a Mother's Day gift.

He thought he had purchased something I would like – but when you're a new mom with a 6-month-old daughter and you're celebrating your first Mother's Day, a professional-quality electric mixer just isn't what you have in mind.

Over time, I realized that giving me a kitchen appliance probably was a reflection of my husband's years of buying gifts for his mother. Come to think of it, she had a mixer just like it.

Since then, my husband and I have learned a lot about Mother's Day. He has learned that when recognizing the vital role played by the mother of his children, a gift that plugs in is not a winner. I have learned to smile while chewing undercooked French toast.

If Mother's Day is a day for pampering mothers, breakfast in bed is the quintessential act of luxury and leisure. Early on, Jim and our children established breakfast in bed as a tradition on this important holiday. They loved the idea of assembling a delectable morning meal on a tray and bringing it to me with a flourish – complete with a Mother's Day fanfare sung to the tune of *Happy Birthday*.

I would sit up in a feigned "just awakened" haze, pretending I hadn't heard the ruckus in the kitchen below that invariably included shouting, tears and an occasional smoke alarm.

My bedridden breakfast feasts – while thoughtful – presented a problem for me because I hate to eat in bed. I even hate the idea of eating in a bedroom. In my mind, there's something incongruous about food and pillows – they just don't go together. And then there's the crumb issue.

A few years ago, I finally let everyone know my true feelings about breakfast in bed. I confessed that I especially don't like eating oatmeal in bed – which, if I recall correctly, was on the menu the morning I let slip my preference for a table with my tableware. So now they call me to the kitchen when their traditional Mother's Day breakfast is ready.

Like the Mother's Day morning meal, the gifts I receive in honor of my maternal role have evolved over the years. Used to be, I could count on tissue-paper floral bouquets and sculptures made of pipe cleaners. I kept these on the kitchen windowsill for the obligatory display period (four days). Within a week, they moved from the kitchen to the top of my dresser to the "file cabinet" under the sink in the bathroom to the permanent off-site storage facility.

Some might call me heartless for sending my Mother's Day gifts to a landfill, but I have four children. There's not enough attic space for all the picture frames made of Popsicle sticks I receive.

Gradually, my Mother's Day gifts became trinkets from the Dollar Store, the one place my children could afford to buy anything. Jim would take all four children shopping on the Saturday before Mother's Day (leaving me at home – alone – which was the real gift). They purchased coffee mugs, hand lotion, oven mitts and jewelry. Of course, jewelry purchased for a dollar discolors my skin, but no matter. It's the thought that counts.

Now that they're older, my children use Mother's Day to buy things they can borrow from me later. I get cool accessories, but I know I won't necessarily be able to find them when I want to wear them, as they'll be hidden in the black hole known as my teenage daughters' bedroom.

Like mothers everywhere, I "ooh" and "aah" on Mother's Day over every act of kindness, every handmade gift, every present wrapped with too much tape and tied with Christmas ribbon. I know the soggy cereal and weak coffee and the cards made of cardboard from the bottom of a shoe box are intended to remind me that I hold a special place in the hearts of my children.

Mother's Day is a great day to be a mom, but what my family doesn't understand is that, despite what the calendar says, Mother's Day doesn't always come on the second Sunday in May.

For me, Mother's Day is a Thursday in April when, after brushing her teeth at bedtime, my second-grader asks, "Mom, which tooth did you say is decaffeinating?" Hiding my laughter so she isn't embarrassed, I explain the tooth that's turning gray "is probably decaying – not decaffeinating" and will be the next to come out.

Mother's Day is also a Saturday in November when, after playing poorly in her last middle-school basketball game, my 13-year-old holds back her tears until we get home and it's OK to melt into my arms and cry out her disappointment.

Mother's Day came 10 years ago in an emergency room, where I held my eldest daughter's hands to my chest and locked her gaze in mine, quelling the fear in my gut as I promised my little girl she would be all right.

Mother's Day came last summer at the end of a brilliant August afternoon, when twilight enveloped the interstate while I drove with my son past endless rows of corn and the sun splattered across the sky and faded into the horizon, and he said out of the blue, "I love you, Mom."

With so many Mother's Days, the gifts I get for being a mom are priceless, indeed.

Marybeth Hicks

Thank you, Lord, for an ordinary day

When the alarm sounds, I awaken to a Friday morning like any other. Rolling slowly to my side, I lift my heavy eyelids toward the digital clock that sits on the night table next to my bed: 6:45.

Every morning, it's the same routine. I hustle out of bed, pack four school lunches, kiss the high schoolers goodbye and then jump in the shower. By 8, I'm ready to drive the younger two children to school. Then it's home for chores – cleaning the kitchen, starting the laundry, running the vacuum and emptying the trash – all completed before 9, my usual target time to begin work in my home office.

This day, I bury my head deeper into my pillow and pull the covers up to my ears.

Not that I can go back to sleep, of course. Mayhem ensues if Mom is the last one up. Rather, I lie in the dark, watching the clock advance the day, minute by reliable minute.

At 7:04, the urge finally strikes me to pull back the blankets. I amble to the kitchen, where it's lights, coffee, action.

By 7:12, our morning routine is well under way. I'm making turkey sandwiches (one with cheese, three without), careful to pack the right fruit in the right bag (two get bananas, one gets an apple, one gets applesauce, but only if it's cinnamon-flavored).

I work around my teenage daughters, who always eat standing up while their overloaded backpacks occupy chairs at the kitchen table.

About 7:29, Amy appears on the scene, still wearing the pajama top and gym shorts she had on when I tucked her into bed last night. She's attempting a stall technique – typical for my 8-year-old.

"Why aren't you dressed for school?" I ask.

"She claims she lost her voice," Betsy interjects.

Working hard to hold back a smile, Amy mouths the words: "It's true. I can't talk." Her lips exaggerate their movements to emphasize each silent syllable.

"We don't have time for your antics. You're going to make us late," I say. "You know the routine. Get moving." I shoo her back upstairs.

"OK, I'll hurry," she says in full voice.

No one remarks on her amazing recovery.

At 7:38, Katie and Betsy head out the door. Within 20 minutes, I'm driving the younger two children to school, steering through our neighborhood and into the pale light of another ordinary day.

Most mornings on the way to school, we talk about the hours ahead. "What are your goals for today?" I'll ask. The answers usually are something like "to get my math done so I don't have homework" (Amy) or "to make it through science without falling asleep" (Jimmy).

This day, though, the ride to school is unusually quiet – and not because Amy's vocal chords have resumed their former phony affliction.

Rather, we're aware of our collective sadness as we drive past our neighbor's house, where an unusual gathering of cars in the driveway reminds us of their extraordinary heartbreak.

Just yesterday, on what should have been a typical Thursday, they lost a son, just 21, to a relentless and ravaging brain tumor. His short life was not to unfold in the ordinary way.

The sympathy that preoccupies my thoughts stays with me on the round trip to school and throughout my morning chores. Eventually, I sit at my desk to answer e-mail and tackle a project that awaits my attention, but I don't get much done.

That I'm blessed to focus on such mundane tasks stirs in me waves of tears for my friend, whose duties today will require surpassing strength and faith – the kind of steely resilience no mother wants to discover she can muster.

Instead of being productive, I mostly spend my time in the awkward awareness that an ordinary day truly is a gift from God.

And so the hours pass until at last it's time to make my way again through the neighborhood to pick up my children from school.

This time, there are even more cars in what seems like an endless line outside my neighbor's home. It's no surprise that a family known for kindness and generosity is being cared for so tenderly by friends and relatives.

Amid the vehicles that crowd the driveway, one catches my eye, and I do a double take. It's a pizza delivery car.

I don't know why, but a sight as incongruous as that pizza car parked outside the home of a grieving family fills me with an odd reassurance.

It strikes me as a simple affirmation that in the midst of a day so exceptionally dark as to be surreal, we all must be fed and nurtured in even the most basic, unremarkable ways.

In the aftermath of a loss so confounding, comfort will be found in the common acts of compassion the family is sure to experience in the weeks and months to come.

I don't know how you could face life's routine rhythm after your reality changes so profoundly.

I don't know how my neighbors will do it.

I only know I'm grateful for the poignant reminder to thank the Lord for every precious day – especially the ordinary ones.

Marybeth Hicks

Marybeth Hicks

Bringing up geeks

Marybeth Hicks

Bringing up geeks

Family night at school comes to its usual end. Children run amok in the gym while parents cluster in circles, holding outerwear for the entire family in a feat known as "the human coat rack."

In this mayhem, I find myself buried under a load of jackets, chatting with another mom. We're making idle small talk about the vagaries of parenting.

At some point in the conversation, I allow as how my children are geeks. I can't honestly recall why I say this, but it's true. I know it. They know it. Everyone who knows them knows it. We're OK with that.

This mom, however, is shocked. "Oh, no," she comforts me. "Your kids are very popular – *really*." She's telling me this as though A) I don't know what it means to be popular; and, B) I want my children to be popular in the first place. (I don't).

I argue the point – with a smile, of course – but I get it pretty quickly that she thinks I am insulting my own children.

"It's OK," I explain. "We like that our kids are geeks." I mean, as long as I'm comfortable with it, why isn't she?

"That just isn't true," she insists. Now she's getting upset with me. This is absurd. What started as a punch line is turning into a discussion about popularity and social status in children. With the load of jackets on my arms and the tension in the air I'm starting to sweat.

I make excuses and a hasty exit, unloading my coat collection as we head out the door. All the while, I'm wondering why it was so important to that mom that my children be popular. What's wrong with bringing up geeks? We're doing it on purpose – and quite successfully, I might add.

The fact is, raising unpopular children takes effort. You spend a lot more time than you might think thwarting the path to a robust social life in the fast lane. Are we sadistically imposing a miserable youth on our offspring, just for the sport of it? Heck no.

We subscribe to the "late bloomer" philosophy, which holds that children who reach the pinnacle of social status by middle school are more at risk. We're eliminating some of the risk with strategic parenting decisions. It takes planning, and it helps to start early – say, in preschool. If you do, you'll be assured a geeky child in middle school and beyond.

For example, when you enroll little Susie or Bobby in preschool, you'll be asked to volunteer for a parent committee. This is a key decision. Whatever you do, don't sign up to plan the class parties. This will put you with the parents of cool, popular children and, by association, your child will be hanging with the A-list before she knows the entire alphabet.

Instead, volunteer for a geek job that involves preschool governance. Write the bylaws for the board. Work on the strategic plan. Best of all, offer to write a grant proposal. You'll be working with just one or two other geek moms and dads, whose children will become your son's or daughter's fast friends. Now you've got the ball rolling.

Before your child gets too old – say, by age 5 – teach him or her to play chess. Also, watch the History Channel together. You just can't beat World War II for geek development.

Once your child learns to read, get him or her to read the newspaper. Also, explain the political process and talk about the headlines over dinner. This assures that your child will answer all the current-events questions in fourth-grade social studies – the sign of a geek in the making.

Next – and this is important – make sure your child is comfortable talking to adults. Geek preteens actually are more comfortable talking to the parents of their peers than to their contemporaries.

When your son or daughter chats about the presidential election cycle while riding home from soccer practice, parents will take notice. They'll mention to their more popular offspring that they're impressed with your child's political savvy. When they do, your risk factors will slide like horn-rimmed glasses on an adolescent nose.

Through the years, you'll have plenty of chances to promote the geek within your child – academic bowl teams, Scout ceremonies, religious milestones. When these events come up, encourage your child to really get into the spirit of the thing. This will keep the cool crowd at a healthy, risk-free distance.

By middle school, all of these tricks will have created a reputation for geekiness that repels invitations to high-risk social functions. You won't need to argue about whether he or she will go to make-out parties, booze bashes and R-rated flicks. That's because there's virtually no chance a teen who reads historical fiction or collects stamps will be invited.

Is it lonely to be a geek? Sure, sometimes, but only for a while. Eventually, your strategy will pay off as your child gravitates to other geeks, who will spend their time together doing safe, geeky things. (Chess club, anyone?)

The trick is to do what we do in our house – be geeky together, as a family. If you cop a sense of humor about your true selves, it's cool.

Of course, if it ever really does become cool to be a geek, we're in trouble.

Marybeth Hicks

But dad, he lives in a pineapple under the sea

T here was no way to avoid it. I needed two replacement smoke alarms, nonfat non-dairy creamer and sidewalk chalk. The bizarre and unrelated nature of my shopping list forced me into the fluorescent green glow of the one-stop big-box superstore.

I'm ambling from hardware through housewares and past the toy department – just across the aisle from beach towels and a display of discount videos – when I hear the unmistakable wailing of a preschooler in distress.

I round the corner on the Lego aisle, and there, holding what appears to be a set of SpongeBob SquarePants action figures, is a boy of about 4. He is crying – no, make that bawling – and begging his father, "Please, Daddy, pleeeeease can I have it?"

Dad glances quickly in my direction, though our eyes don't meet. I keep my pace toward electronics as I hear him say, "Maybe for your birthday."

His little son piles it on: "Please, please, please Daddy." The child is relentless.

The boy's begging causes some sort of chemical reaction in my brain. I nearly stop in my tracks and head back to the toy department to buy the action figures for him myself. Then I overhear his dad's tone of voice change sharply. "No," he says.

That's all I hear because the sound of his fatherly retort is muffled by racks of exercise clothes.

Immediately I'm proud of this father and baffled by the readiness of my sympathy for his little boy. Children who cry for what they want usually repel me.

I think it was the begging – as if the action figures were the little boy's lifeline, his last, best hope for happiness. The boy was convincing; I have to give it to him.

So what makes a 4-year-old boy so intent on owning rubber replicas of Sponge-Bob, Patrick, Squidward and Mr. Krebs?

As long as I'm pondering this question, here's another: Why does my 7-year-old daughter think our dog would look cute in a Prada dog collar (assuming there is such a thing, which she swears there must be "for Paris Hilton's dog")?

The quick answer is television, of course. According to TV-Turnoff Network, a nonprofit organization that encourages children and adults to watch much less television in order to promote healthier lives and communities (www.tvturnoff.org), children view roughly 40,000 television commercials per year, developing brand loyalty by age 2. Ninety-seven percent of American children younger than 6 own products based on TV shows or movies, which means the relationship between viewing and purchasing goes well beyond traditional advertising.

The dad at the superstore could confirm the strength of this marketing tactic.

Yet television alone can't explain why middle-school lockers from coast to coast house purses made by designers Downey & Bourke or Louis Vuitton or why those handbags are holding iPods and MAC makeup and Coach wallets and Motorola flip phones with built-in cameras.

Not all middle school lockers are full of such pricey products – not my daughter's, anyway. Nevertheless, there is enough consumerism in children to convince me we're raising a generation of people who think they are what they own.

Case in point: My youngest daughter needed sneakers. She loves the color pink, so I picked out the only pair of pink-and-white shoes I could find that looked sturdy and comfortable. She tried them on, hopped across the shoe department, claimed they made her jump higher than the old shoes and pronounced them suitable.

I paid for the shoes and – as is our custom – she wore them out of the store, the old pair having been tossed into the trash bin under the cash register.

It turned out the shoes I bought for my second-grader were made by Phat Farm, a company that says its products are "born out of the hip-hop lifestyle." According to one of my older daughter's friends, those sneakers "make a statement," though what that statement might be, I can't say.

I know this for certain: If my children are on the cutting edge of hip, it's probably by accident.

On the other hand, my eighth-grade daughter would love to own an iPod. "Everybody" has one, while she still uses a personal CD player that requires her to carry a stash of compact discs. An iPod would hold 5,000 songs (read "which you, Mom, could buy for me on iTunes.") This is an item I'm not likely to purchase accidentally.

It's not that I think she's exaggerating. There do seem to be an awful lot of children walking around with $300 worth of digital music players in their pockets. In fact, after a recent school function, I stayed behind to help clean up and found someone's iPod left carelessly on the floor of a classroom. "Who leaves an iPod player on the floor and walks away?" I asked.

"Someone who didn't pay for it," another mom said. And there's the rub.

It's hard to say "no" when children ask for things, but it's the only way to teach them to delay gratification, earn what they own and be responsible. Of course, it's easier if you start in the toy department when they're little.

That superstore dad may have had lots of reasons for saying "no" to the SpongeBob set. Perhaps he didn't have the money to buy it; perhaps his son already has a toy box full of rubber figurines; perhaps he just loathes the idea of a talking sponge who wears trousers.

Whatever the reason, his decision reflected a belief it was better to say "no" than to give in to the urgent desire of a child's frenzied consumerism. You go, Dad.

　　　　　　　　　Marybeth Hicks

Bad parents bug my pest guy

W hen the doorbell rings, it's all I can do to pull myself out of the chair and walk to the front hall. Reaching for the Kleenex® box has sapped all my energy, and now, holding my head upright is causing my sinuses to flood. By the time I reach the door, I have to sneeze the word "Hello" to Bert, my pest-control man.

"You're sick," he says, stating the obvious.

"Yeah, one of my kids brought a disease home from school," I explain.

Bert pumps his bug juicer a few times and then starts simultaneously spraying and talking. He hasn't been here in a month, so we have a lot of catching up to do.

"So, we both have high school seniors this year," I say. "How's your daughter doing so far?"

Bert and I often compare notes on rearing teenage girls. Usually he laments her choices of friends and activities.

"Well, she's not pregnant."

Yikes. This is just a Friday morning bug visit, and what with my plugged nasal passages and the cloud remaining in my brain from last night's antihistamines, I'm not too quick on the uptake.

"Um ... is that something you're concerned about?" When in doubt, ask a question.

Bert goes on to explain that three of his daughter's closest friends "turned up pregnant" over the summer, a development about which he's appalled. He has decided his measure of success for his daughter's senior year is to assure that the only tests she takes are in school and not in an obstetrician's office.

"The thing that slays me is that these 17-year-old girls are happy and excited. They can't wait to be mommies." He shakes his head as he moves to the kitchen on a quest for pests.

Sadly, Bert has concluded he's the only parent in his daughter's social sphere who "has a clue." For example, last spring, he was the only one to object to a hotel room on prom night.

He's the only one who said "no" when his daughter asked to go on a spring-break cruise with a group of girls and one mom as a chaperone. ("How the heck is one mom going to supervise a dozen teenagers on a cruise ship?")

He was alone in his fight against his daughter's decision to have her nose pierced. Even Bert's wife threw up her hands on that one with the rationale, "At least it's not a tattoo."

According to Bert, teenage motherhood is the obvious result of the permissive and complacent parenting going on around him. He looks at me in confusion and says, "What are these people thinking?"

Indeed.

Most of the time, we work ourselves into a conversational lather as Bert tells me the latest episodes in his parenting saga, but today, I'm too sick to get my ire up the way I usually do.

"I guess we're just 'old school,'" I say, shaking my head in congested agreement as I shuffle back to the den to watch TV.

Picking up the remote, I begin my search for suitable sick-day entertainment, all the while thinking about the cultural shift that has permitted a measure of teenage success to become "She's not pregnant."

At about that moment, my channel surfing lands on Janet Jackson's new video. Seeing it surprises me for a couple of reasons.

First, I thought we had blocked all the music-video channels from our television, but apparently we missed one at the top of the dial, and second, Janet is revisiting the "wardrobe malfunction" she debuted at the Super Bowl a few years ago

This time, though, there is no mistake. Janet's pornographic lyrics and coarse choreography are punctuated intentionally by flashes of her bare breasts.

I watch this "artistic" rendition of a song called *So Excited,* and even in my foggy state of consciousness, it's obvious to me that Bert is up against a whole lot more than just the permissive parents at his daughter's high school.

He's up against the Janet Jacksons of the world – the people who make lots of money selling sex to teens through music, movies, TV shows and magazines.

A dad with a strong set of values to pass along to his daughter is no match for the constant barrage of media messages about what constitutes desirable behavior, not to mention the inertia of adults who let the culture set their children's moral standards.

Then again, despite the odds that the culture will win the war, my money's on Bert (and not just because he has a successful track record against pests of all varieties).

The reason I think Bert will prevail and ultimately will help his daughter toward responsible adulthood is because he won't leave it alone.

He still talks to his daughter about her choices and doesn't shy away from the tough questions and unpleasant conversations.

He still gets mad when other parents throw up their hands and declare they can't control their teens.

He's still incredulous about the provocative way girls dress and the poor manners he sees in teenage boys.

He still expects his daughter to comply with his rules as long as she's living in his house.

In short, Bert is proof that "old school" dads are still out there.

Marybeth Hicks

Naked guy sells more than jeans

"Oh my gosh, Mom, look at that." Betsy nearly shoved my appendix into my spine with her elbow as she nudged me into the glass wall outside the Abercrombie and Fitch store inside our suburban shopping mall.

I started to ask why she was breaking my ribs to get my attention, when suddenly the image that startled her nearly knocked me into the kiosk that sells *Dippin' Dots,* the 21st century "ice cream product."

"Yikes," I said.

"Yuck," Betsy answered.

We maneuvered quickly to keep 8-year-old Amy from noticing the larger-than-life poster leaning against the wall at the entrance to the Abercrombie and Fitch store, since I figured she might ask why the body (no face) of a mostly-naked guy was covering the wall of a clothing store.

Fortunately, Amy was easily distracted by the gumballs just beyond the offending in-store display. But I couldn't get my mind off the rude photograph and the larger issue it represents. The more we walked and talked and shopped, the madder I got.

Just what was so offensive in the A&F window? A black-and-white "glamour" shot of a shirtless, male torso, wearing only unzipped bluejeans with the belt hanging open. The jeans are worn so low as to reveal a good portion of his physique, and the implication about what's going on inside the jeans is clear.

I'm not sure if this photo sells jeans to teens, but I do know it's selling them something.

If you don't know, Abercrombie and Fitch is a national chain that bills itself as a "lifestyle" retailer (whatever that means), and is part of a corporate family that includes three other similar brands. They sell clothes for preteens, teens and young adults – trendy styles that look good only on people whose bodies have yet to form hips – and their retail locations are notable for their loud, thumping, music and racy window photographs.

The store was actually founded in 1892 as a sporting goods retailer for wealthy hunters and outdoorsmen. Teddy Roosevelt was a big Abercrombie customer, as were most presidents through Gerald Ford, which was about the time the business started to flounder.

But no longer. It's been reinvented to respond to young consumers with a taste for low-rise denim jeans, body-hugging tops for gals, and the studied casual look for guys that says "I paid a lot for a shirt that wrinkles easily." Abercrombie clothes are expensive, too, but admittedly that may be just the opinion of a mom who won't pay $49 for a T-shirt.

Back to the mall. Betsy, Amy and I manage to traverse the shopping center without another face-to-torso encounter, but I'm so irked by the audacity of this display I can't let it go. "Bets," I say quietly, "take Amy toward the exit and wait for me. I'm going to make a fuss."

Betsy has seen me make a fuss once or twice before and she knows it won't be pretty, so she gladly grabs Amy by the hand and walks the other way.

For the record, I had no intention of ranting; I just wanted to tell someone associated with the company that I thought their display poster was inappropriate, especially in a store that sells to youngsters.

I headed back to the Abercrombie entrance, passing "naked boy" as I looked for the manager, who listened attentively as I expressed my concerns. Long story short – she gave me the toll-free number for Customer Service and said my complaint would go unheeded unless I went on record as objecting to the store display. My "fuss" would have to wait a day.

By now I had committed myself to take a stand, so the next day I called the company and got an automated menu, "Press 1 to place a catalog order; press 2 if you have an issue with a retail store." Hmmm. An "issue"? Seems like they may get these calls a lot.

At last, someone named Ryan took my call and I articulated my concerns:

A. Abercrombie markets to teens and preteens;

B. Their in-store photo displays use nudity to send strong sexual messages to youngsters – namely, that buying Abercrombie products will make them sexy and will promote their sex lives;

C. It's morally abhorrent to corrupt the innocence of children to make a buck selling blue jeans; and,

D. Assuming there even is a line to cross in our culture when it comes to marketing, they crossed it.

Ryan – who let me know he isn't authorized to speak for the company – told me the goal of the display photos is "to draw attention to the store, good or bad." Then he gave me the name and number of the store's Director of Customer Service/Vice President of Public Relations. (I left several voice-mail messages informing him I'd be writing a column on this topic and asking for his comment; he never responded.)

So I guess that's it, then. My complaint has been duly noted by the efficient and respectful Ryan, who I hope was fully clothed while we spoke, but since it's Abercrombie we're talking about, who knows?

According to the only person from Abercrombie I could get to comment, albeit unofficially, the photos are intended to get attention of any sort – a goal I clearly have accomplished for the "lifestyle retailer" – and still "naked boy" graces the main intersection of my shopping mall.

I guess they got the best of me.

Then again, parents like me can always speak up by closing our wallets to the "lifestyle" they're selling at Abercrombie.

It's only money, of course, but it might be enough to get their attention.

Marybeth Hicks

Maybe it's just me

FIVE
SIX
SEVEN
EIGHT...

Amy stands in the second row on the end. She's wearing blue sweat pants and a pink shirt. Her hair is swept up into the ponytail that looked neater this morning. Her hands have streaks of magic marker on them. Her face is not quite clean.

Still, back there in the second row, she looks perfectly put together as the teacher calls out "a-five-six-seven-eight" to signal the start of the dance combination.

It's parent observation day in the studio. The dozen girls in Amy's musical theater class show off their newfound skills, acting out emotions and belting show tunes at the top of their little lungs. It's too cute.

Unfortunately, I can't really concentrate on Amy and her fellow thespians-in-training. All I can focus on are the two children behind me whose abominable behavior is multiplied by the fact that they are reflected in the mirror on the opposite wall.

There's just enough space between the last row of chairs and the wall behind us for them to run back and forth from one end of the room to the other. The 5-year-old sister of one of the girls in the class has engaged the interest of someone else's 9-year-old brother, and together they're entertaining each other until their designated time as "tag-alongs" is up.

The problem is, the entertainment is supposed to be out on the dance floor. Instead of sitting quietly with their parents to watch the singers and dancers, these two would-be audience members are jumping, thumping and even whooping as they play an impromptu game of tag.

I turn my head just enough to look over my right shoulder. I send a look to no one in particular that says, "If those are your kids, you might want to settle them down." Then I turn back to watch Amy and her classmates.

The behavior behind me doesn't stop. Instead, it's turning into a stage-whispered ruckus. Again I turn back. Again I look generally over the group of parents. Again I send a glance that says, "Hey, folks, if those are your kids, you might want to think about a lasso."

A few more bars of music, and still the rowdy pair behind me continue their antics. With plywood flooring beneath their feet, their running sounds like an army battalion marching through the room. I'm exaggerating only a little here.

I decide a dirty look is in order, but this time, when I turn my head, I realize I can't glare at the parents of these two children because I can't figure out which of the adults in the chairs around me are their parents. All the adults in the room are facing forward, intently watching the girls perform their dance steps.

There's a Stepford quality to this moment. I ask myself, "Is it me?" Perhaps I'm the only person who expects children to sit quietly and watch their siblings during a performance.

Granted, we're not in an auditorium, and the lights are not dimmed for a major debut. Nevertheless, the assumption is that the parents and family members in attendance came to observe the performers on the dance floor, not their misbehaving siblings in the back of the room.

This kind of thing happens more and more. I'm not sure if poor behavior is actually on the rise or if my own children are at long last old enough to behave appropriately – mostly – and so I'm finally able to notice what's going on around me.

What I'm noticing is a whole bunch of parents doing nothing.

No "shushing" or whispered admonitions to sit still. No warning glances or shoulder taps. Not even a wry smile as if to say, "Just because you're adorable doesn't mean it's OK to be disruptive."

There seems to be a pervasive attitude that rude behavior in children is to be expected and tolerated, which brings me back to the question, "Is it me?"

I don't want to get used to rude children.

I don't tolerate it when my own children behave thoughtlessly in public, and I don't see why I should put up with it when other people's children run amok. I haven't figured out yet what to do other than send a series of progressively more irritated glances toward the adults whose job it is to react – which obviously doesn't work, if my experience at the dance studio is any indication.

With the song-and-dance exhibition nearing an end, the mother of the energetic little girl reels her daughter in with an index finger and pats the chair next to her. This prompts the boy to plop down against the back wall and pick up a Game Boy to kill the time that's left. Apparently, watching his sister perform a show tune is a fate worse than death.

On the way home, I congratulate Amy and tell her how proud I am of her efforts, especially in the face of such a boisterous back row. "You really stayed in character and stayed focused, even with those kids running back and forth behind the seats."

"What kids?" she asks.

"There were two children playing tag all during the class while you and your friends showed the parents the routines you're learning. I thought their behavior was rude and unacceptable. You didn't notice them?"

"Nope."

OK, so maybe it is just me.

Marybeth Hicks

Christmas shopping lands me in the laundry

Most of the time, I try hard to ignore advertising, but at this time of year, that's not easy to do. With Christmas only a week away, retailers saturate the media with pitches for "the perfect gift for that special someone." You can't escape it.

Over the course of the holiday season, I keep a mental list of the ads that take the Christmas spirit to new extremes.

For example, there's an ad for a furniture store that suggests, "This year, decorate for the holidays with leather." It goes on to list the price for a new sofa, love seat and ottoman. Apparently, just putting up a tree is no longer enough to deck the halls.

The ad that really says "Peace on Earth," though, is the one for the adult superstore. Playing the tune *Santa Baby* in the background, this commercial walks the consumer through a steamy scenario: "Has the spark gone out of your relationship with old St. Nick? Why not create Christmas magic with a gift of lingerie?"

It's odd and really uncomfortable to think about shopping at an adult superstore to celebrate the birth of the Baby Jesus.

Of course, most of the ads are directed at children, designed to reach parent-consumers via their offspring's relentless begging and pleading.

When I see these ads, I'm glad my children are growing older and I'm no longer buying gifts for preschoolers. The choices are intimidating.

On the one hand, there are computer systems for small children that promote learning and fun. They introduce technology to teach phonics, math and geography, yet they make education feel more like play.

But some of the technology that's out there seems less educational and more – what's the term I'm looking for? – self-absorbed.

Exhibit: The device that puts a camera on top of your television set and transmits images of your child onto the TV screen. (Some savvy toy inventors are going to make lots of money this season because they realized children love to look at themselves on security cameras.)

It's sad to imagine a 4-year-old standing in front of the TV entertaining himself with images of – himself. Then again, you could buy one of those "Happy Bunny"

T-shirts to go with this gift that says, "It's all about me. Deal with it."

When they were little, it was easy to delight my children on Christmas morning simply by wrapping a few coloring books and a new package of crayons. In addition to a stocking filled with candy canes and a toothbrush (Santa was always into dental hygiene), everyone got a pair of pajamas, a doll or a truck and a few books.

Generating an enthusiastic response gets harder as they get older, thanks in part to the expectations retailers create.

By the looks of the advertisements, Christmas is not just a time for giving, it's a time for giving big, expensive electronics and gobs of cool gifts that scatter all over the living room floor. I find myself defensively reminding my children, "Even Jesus got only three presents, you know."

With all the options out there for gift giving, I realized this year, for the first time, that I don't know for sure what my children might like.

No, wait. Not all my children. Amy is just 8, so she's been telling me what she wants for Christmas since about Labor Day. The other three haven't given many clues about what they hope to find under the tree.

My uncertainty prompted me to do something I've never done before: I encouraged them to make Christmas lists. It's contrary to my belief that a gift is not something one orders like food in a restaurant, but I was stymied.

Unfortunately, the lists didn't give me the hoped-for guidance. Jimmy wrote down a few items I probably won't buy. (I'm protesting the collection of yet more Yu-Gi-Oh cards on the belief that enough is enough.)

Katie's list says "books." No details.

Betsy's list says "anything." Either she'll really be happy with whatever she receives or she wants so many different items there's no point in listing them all.

Time is running out. With only a week to go, neither their lists nor the incessant media advertisements have inspired me to make the dreaded trip to the shopping mall, and the idea of simply wandering around until something hits me sounds both expensive and exhausting.

So, rather than look outside my home for ideas, I do the one thing that always inspires me to think about my children.

I fold laundry.

Standing in the kitchen, I stack their T-shirts, socks and gym shorts in four neat piles across the table. I let my mind drift from child to child in the same way their sweatshirts and blue jeans and school uniforms mingle in the basket.

I reflect on their interests and passions.

I remind myself of what I know about their dreams and desires.

I recall things they've mentioned in passing; I think about what's in their hearts.

By the time I finish sorting and folding and ironing their clothes, I have a plan, and I'm ready to head to the store.

All of a sudden, I can't wait for Christmas morning.

Marybeth Hicks

Daughter imparts advice for cool parents

"**M**om, can I borrow some paper? I've decided to write a book."

This is encouraging. I have just spent an entire summer forcing Amy to read in half-hour increments, time she mostly spent updating me on her progress one page at a time. Amy is a reluctant reader, just as she is a reluctant eater of vegetables and a reluctant brusher of teeth.

I'm thinking my constant harping about reading finally is paying off in a new affection for all things literary. "You're writing a book? What's it about?" I ask.

Perhaps reading Laura Ingalls Wilder's *Little House in the Big Woods* has her interested in historical fiction. Or maybe she's been inspired by Anne Mazer's *Amazing Days of Abbey Hayes* series to write a contemporary story about a girl like herself.

"I'm writing an advice book for kids," she says.

I might have known.

"What kind of advice are you going to offer?" I try to hide the suspicion in my voice.

"Well ...." She takes a breath and puts one hand on her hip. "You know how you are always giving parents advice on how to raise their kids to be geeks? I'm going to give kids advice on how to make their parents cool."

She grabs more paper than she needs from the computer printer, reaches for the box of art supplies in my supply closet and goes to work, leaving me to wonder: "Is she writing from personal experience or wishful thinking?"

Being cool is important to Amy, which is ironic, given the parenting philosophy my husband and I employ.

Long ago, we realized that children who are "geeks" seem more innocent and less cynical than "cool kids." Without the burden of maintaining a cool image, geeks are free to enjoy the History Channel, playing chess with Grandpa, collecting rocks and pretending to be mad scientists with their own chemistry sets.

We've worked hard as parents to assure that our children aren't able to live a cool lifestyle. This isn't as easy as it sounds, because children can graze on "the culture of cool" the way cows graze on grass. It's everywhere.

Still, our goal is to promote substance over style, innocence over exploitation and a genuine experience of childhood instead of a short period as miniature adults.

Admittedly, achieving the goal of raising geeks may be easier for us than for some people. Jim was co-captain of the Academic Bowl team in high school, and I developed an early and outspoken interest in politics. Our gene pool is predisposed to the development of news junkies who spout trivia, two hallmarks of being a geek.

Nevertheless, geek genes aren't enough in a culture as cool as 21st-century America, so we also shelter our children to the extent we're able. This way, they have time to grow into their own personalities and interests before cultural barometers such as Nickelodeon's Kids' Choice Awards tell them how to behave and what trends to follow.

In fact, I thought we were doing a pretty good job of imparting our geek values to our children – until I read the first draft of Amy's book.

Here is Amy's advice for children to train their parents to be cool:

Step No. 1: Get them some cool shades.

Step No. 2: Sequins. (Apparently no elaboration is necessary.)

Step No. 3: Get them some "bling."

Step No. 4: Fill them in on trends.

Step No. 5: Help them when it's time to shop. (Illustration of hip clothes.)

Step No. 6: Tell them to say things that are cool. (Example, "Yo!")

(Sigh).

Step No. 7: Update them on fashion. (Clearly my daughter doesn't like the way I dress.)

Step No. 8: Tell them to wear black. (Duh. Even a geek mom knows to wear black.)

Step No. 9: Tell them what's in. (Isn't this the same as Step No. 4?)

Step No. 10: Tell them not to try too hard.

I'm picturing myself ambling the aisles of the grocery store, wearing sunglasses, "bling" and the latest pencil-legged jeans with the trendiest stiletto heels, saying things like, "Yo, deli guy, can I please have some shaved ham?"

Yet I'm not supposed to try too hard?

I decide it's better to encourage Amy's interest in writing than to discourage her preoccupation with the culture of cool.

"This is a great book," I tell Amy after reading it. "I especially like the pictures and the way you used my metallic silver marker on all the pages."

It's obvious I have work to do in helping my youngest child develop her own sense of individuality. Her advice book suggests more than a passing interest in one's appearance as an important facet of self-esteem.

Or maybe she just thinks I need a makeover. Hard to say.

She bounds out of the room to find a three-ring binder for her book. I decide to suggest she write a story about a mom and daughter going on a shopping trip – better to ease her into fiction with something she's passionate about rather than dismiss her ideas as trite. (She does have a point about wearing black, after all.)

Besides, I'm not really worried that Amy is destined for life in the fast lane.

At the tender age of 8, she may be a fashion maven, but deep inside beats the heart of a geek.

Marybeth Hicks

Pulling the plug for better etiquette

"**W**hat is that hanging from your ear?" I ask. Glancing into the rearview mirror, I can see only the right edge of my daughter's face and a thin, gray wire hanging in her hair.

But of course, I'm not really asking, "What is it?"

I'm asking, "Why is an ear-bud headphone in one ear while you are engaged in conversation with other human beings?"

"I can hear you perfectly, Mom," Katie answers defensively. She can see where this is going.

Whether she can hear me perfectly is not my issue. This is not a long car trip on which I permit my children to plug into their personal music devices to pass the time. It's a 10-minute drive to the doctor's office for flu shots, offering us a chance to catch up about the busy school day and get a handle on the homework load for the evening.

"I may not have mentioned this before, but wandering around the planet with an ear bud in your head is rude," I say. "I know kids do it all the time, but it's bad manners unless you're alone and you don't expect to talk to people."

"Good point," she says as she stuffs the cord in her pocket. "Besides, I don't really know how my friends do this. I keep thinking I'm going to answer your questions by repeating the song lyrics."

In today's culture of "cool," a single ear-bud headphone placed in one ear is typical for teens. This leaves the other ear open to take cell-phone calls. Really cool teens even have personal digital assistants – PDAs – to connect to the Internet and e-mail no matter where they go.

All of this technology is designed for communication. Teens keep in touch with instant messages, text messages, voice messages and photo messages. They even have developed code languages to help them transmit information quickly, without using actual words (LOL – laugh out loud).

However, if the conversations I hear between my children and their friends are any indication, all this technology may be robbing some young people of the ability to talk. What we've gained in immediacy we've lost in polite conversation.

Case in point: One day last summer, Betsy invited a friend to spend the afternoon at our house. We drove to her home to pick her up, and when she climbed into the car, my daughter initiated a friendly conversation.

"How's your summer going?

"Fine." (Not, "Fine, how about yours?" Just "fine.")

"What have you been doing?" Betsy tried again.

"Nothing." (Not, "Nothing. What about you?" Just "nothing.")

"Do you have anything fun planned?" I had to give Betsy credit. She wasn't giving up.

"No." (Not "No, but stop asking me so many stupid questions," though that's what it sounded like from the driver's seat.)

Clearly, it was going to be a long day.

Sure enough, after several attempts to engage in activities that would require the polite participation of her guest (board games, a bike ride, baking brownies), Betsy suggested they watch a movie. Who could blame her? It's hard to spend a whole day with someone who doesn't talk.

If conversational skills among young peers are on the decline, getting children to talk to an adult is like cracking a bank vault.

Not long ago, Jimmy invited a new friend to play at our house for the first time. Because I didn't know him, I tried to talk to him while making the boys' lunch. I asked how he likes school, inquired about his favorite classes and teachers and what sports he likes best. To every question, he replied, "I don't know" while staring blankly at my kitchen floor.

Now, I realize it's not always comfortable for a 12-year-old boy to chat amiably with the mother of his friend, but I wasn't asking deeply personal questions that would put him in the conversational hot seat.

The sad reality is, I don't think anyone has taught this boy how to engage in polite conversation. Unfortunately, his rude behavior convinced me he's not a child I want hanging around our house. He hasn't been back since then.

Loads of great books and Web sites are available to help parents teach rules of etiquette – so many that it may seem like a daunting task. We have simplified this effort in our house by remembering that all manners are about making other people feel respected and comfortable – about putting the feelings of others ahead of ourselves.

Not that there aren't a few rules worth passing along, such as to look at the person speaking to you; answer a question politely; demonstrate respect for adults in conversation; say "please," "thank you" and "excuse me." Even a 5-year-old can master the basics if parents take the time to teach and practice polite behavior.

Then again, once these fundamentals are well-learned, you can tackle the more advanced rules for participating in polite society – rules that include: "Take that silly ear bud out of your ear while I'm speaking to you. Please."

Marybeth Hicks

Space reserved for rude drivers only

A t the risk of oversimplification, here's what's wrong with the world today: bad manners.

Bad manners are the source of wars, gang violence, political scandal, road rage and marital disputes. Bad manners mean bad customer service, bad neighborhoods, even bad breath.

Case in point: the superstore parking lot, where I wait and wander in a quest for a space to beach the van. It's a Saturday, so I'm not eager to join the throngs of shoppers looking for lawn furniture, new bikes and flip flops in one convenient stop, but I have a list and an hour set aside for errands.

At the risk of behaving like a stalker, I wait by the store's exit doors for departing shoppers who might lead me to a potential parking space. A stealthy and experienced parking-lot scout, I know this strategy doesn't always work. Some folks lead you down aisle A only to cut through a row of cars to their vehicle, inconveniently parked in aisle B. By the time you get to the actual location of the open space, it's too late.

Not this time. I see a happy shopper heading out to the parking lot. Her car is about halfway down the aisle. I follow her, giving her a smile and a wave while I wait for her to load a cart full of items into her trunk. My turn signal indicates my intent to occupy her parking space.

I have left plenty of room for the driver of the departing car to maneuver – more space than she needs, in fact – an act of good manners. The next thing I know, a car at the end of the aisle ahead of me backs up, stopping just short of my front bumper.

"She's got to be kidding," I mutter. "This woman can't possibly be planning to park in my spot. I'm sitting here with my blinker on."

I honk the horn politely at first – a slight "beep beep" to attract her attention.

She sticks her arm out the window and flags me to go around her. The audacity of this woman is astounding.

"Unbelievable," I say incredulously. This time I lay on the horn long and loud but the poacher doesn't budge. Next thing I know, the woman loading her shopping bags slams her trunk and makes a hasty exit (no doubt avoiding the possibility she'll play the role of "innocent victim" in this scenario) and Parking Space Poacher zips into the vacancy.

I'm stunned at this display of brashness and bad manners. More than stunned – I'm hopping mad. I inch forward and flail my hands in an effort to show her I'm upset. She puts her head down, busying herself inside her car until I drive away.

Meanwhile, the owner of the car in the space next to hers arrives, quickly backs out and drives away. Justice is mine.

I park my van and walk into the superstore a few feet behind the poacher. "That was really rude," I say.

"There was plenty of room to go around me," poacher says.

"I was obviously waiting for that parking space," I say. "I had my blinker on."

"Sorry," she says sarcastically, disappearing into the racks of clothes just inside the store.

"Actually, you're not," I say under my breath. Grrrr.

I'm not exactly proud of my reaction. Usually when this kind of thing happens to me, I smile and offer a silent prayer that the inconsiderate buffoon offending me will have a moment of enlightenment. I tend to give people the benefit of the doubt.

A truism about bad manners is: They're contagious.

Teaching good manners to children probably was easier when more people practiced them. Unfortunately, polite society has devolved to such a degree that we're mostly surrounded by examples of what not to do.

("Son, do you see that young man wearing his pants below his hips with his underwear exposed? He's spewing vulgar language at the girls across the street while tossing his trash on the ground and blowing cigarette smoke into the faces of his friends. Don't do that when you grow up.")

Not that my manners are always exemplary. Fortunately, my children often miss the irony of being told to remove their elbows from the table by a woman with corn flakes in her mouth.

Still, teaching good manners is one way to give children a leg up in the adult world. Simple habits such as looking at the person to whom they're speaking, using people's names in conversation ("I'm fine, Mrs. Smith. How are you?"), saying "please" and "thank you," or holding a door for an elder are so uncommon as to be remarkable.

Not to mention, teaching good manners to children is one of the few things for which a parent actually can take credit.

Good looks? God's work.

Intelligence? Nature, not nurture.

Perfect pitch?

Double jointedness?

Photographic memory?

Sheer luck.

Manners, on the other hand, can be taught, a reminder of which I enjoyed recently when someone commented – again – on the mature and articulate way in which my daughter answered the phone and recorded a message.

Whether she remembers to deliver the phone message is another issue.

Then again, after I make my apologies for rudely neglecting to return the call in a timely fashion, it's nice to hear that my daughter practiced what I preached.

Marybeth Hicks

Barbie's not my scene

Way cool...?

One of the best things about having a cellular phone is getting into the car after grocery shopping, calling my house and instructing one of my children to turn on the oven. This cuts about eight minutes off the time it takes to get frozen lasagna on the table.

"Preheat the oven to 400 degrees," I say to Katie as I load the bags of food into the van.

"OK, but there's a problem," she says. I hear the electronic beeping of the oven dial in the background.

"There's a problem with the oven?" I ask.

"No, with the TV. Nickelodeon is playing the new My Scene movie, and when I told Amy to turn it off, things got ugly around here," she explains.

"Say no more." I brace myself for the inevitable whining and begging I will face from Amy, my 8-year-old fashionista, when I walk into my house.

Barbie is her barometer of style, and *My Scene Goes Hollywood* is Barbie's new animated movie adventure. This is the first full-length feature based on the My Scene doll collection, but as my older daughter correctly guessed, it is not a movie I would allow.

In case you don't know, My Scene is Barbie's new milieu. Having long ago dumped the antiquated and uncool Midge and Ken for hip girls including Chelsea, Madison and Delancey and guys named Hudson, River, Ellis and Sutton (all names that suggest the question, "Do the creators of these characters ever get out of Manhattan?"), Barbie underwent a complete makeover from glamour icon to urban trendsetter. She has become "way cool," according to Amy.

Unfortunately, being "cool" is what makes My Scene off limits for my daughter. This is because "cool" means immodestly attired, boy-obsessed and media-saturated. Barbie's values seem intact (she's unfailingly kind, puts her friends first and serves as the voice of responsibility among her crowd), but her lifestyle is everything I'm trying to teach my third-grader to avoid.

Not that Barbie and the My Scene characters are the most objectionable of today's fashion dolls. That distinction would go to Bratz, a collection of dolls that appear to have collagen-injected lips to offset their eyeliner tattoos. The manufacturer claims the Bratz motto is "the only girls with the passion for fashion," but this is true only if fashion includes stilettos.

I'm not kidding. Just go the Bratz Web site (www.bratzpack.com) and check the page titled *Flaunt it! Or Forget it!* Just to be sure girls who visit the site don't get confused about what's cool, *Flaunt it!* offers this fashion advice: "Express your rock style by wearing denim fitted jacket, knee-high stiletto boots, vintage concert tee, hair with highlights and lowlights."

The page also helpfully tells girls what to avoid: "True rockers would never wear: pastels, butterflies, capri pants, flower prints, mesh Chinese slippers and glow necklaces" (whatever those are).

Did I mention this is Internet content based on a line of dolls? For children? I didn't know you could buy stilettos for children.

I'm convinced our culture puts too low a value on childhood innocence. Otherwise, why would the Web site for Barbie's My Scene movie explain in a story synopsis on its Web site (www.myscene.com) which animated characters from the movie are "hot" and who is "crushing" on whom? The very notion that my child might use the word "hot" to describe anything other than the temperature in July makes me cringe.

A growing body of evidence clearly confirms that our children absorb the messages transmitted in the pervasive media they encounter for roughly a quarter of their waking hours, from television shows and commercials to movies, Internet sites and electronic games. The attitudes and behaviors depicted in the media can serve as strong examples of what the culture promotes as normal and appropriate and even admirable.

My Scene Goes Hollywood is none of those. It's a cartoon movie about a group of hyperconsumers whose greatest fantasy – going to Hollywood – becomes a melodramatic reality. As a morality play, it boldly states that if you find success but begin to think you're "all that," your friends will be annoyed with you.

The more I learn, the more I believe insidious influences such as *My Scene Goes Hollywood* will erode my daughter's innocence unless I build a hedge of protection around her. Given the pervasive presence of media (dolls that beget TV shows that beget Web sites that beget movies), that hedge needs to be pretty high, but sheltering my children from some of what the media offer is an exercise in parenting that is worth my best effort.

I'm thinking about this huge cultural conundrum as I unload the groceries from my van. Any moment, I expect to hear Amy's side of the My Scene debate, when I'll be faced once again with explaining why it's not something we allow at our house.

But thank goodness, she already has headed outside to join the neighborhood children playing football across the street. So much for Barbie.

Marybeth Hicks

The morning after Santa

Biblically speaking, the Christmas season has just begun. Traditionally, today is the second day of Christmas, on which we might expect to receive "two turtle doves." Though, what we might do with them isn't clear.

With 10 more days until the Epiphany, we ought to be toasting the season with a little wassail and spreading Christmas cheer as we visit friends and relatives, waiting for the arrival of the Three Wise Men.

But the garbage bags full of wrapping paper in my garage tell another story. Christmas appears to be officially over.

We can't go visiting anyway. Everyone we know went to the mall to shop the after Christmas sales. The really savvy gift givers are returning the items they purchased on Christmas Eve and repurchasing them, just to get back the difference in savings.

Sadly, Santa himself is probably in the return line, taking back the Beatles retrospective four-disc compilation that even the most retro teen found repugnant.

Christmas morning might have been a disappointment this year. That's because the only child left in my house who sits on Santa's lap pulled a fast one during her audience with the elf.

It was just a couple of weeks ago that we managed to fit in our traditional trip to the mall for haircuts and a visit with Big Man in the Red Suit. We're standing in the rope line that winds itself behind the photographer's kiosk, where, for only $29.95, you can have a 3x5-inch laser photo of your child with Santa. If you want St. Nick to look pleasant, it's an extra $7.99.

We're waiting and chatting, chatting and waiting. This is the moment when anything is possible – the cadre of potential toys and treasures is limitless. My daughter bats around the variety of things she could mention to Santa Claus.

We manage to avoid questions about how Santa makes name-brand toys and whether you have to send things back to the North Pole if they break, or just take them to Toys R Us for a refund.

At last, we're near the front of the line. Only one little girl waits ahead of us. But what's this? Santa rises from his throne, grabs his sack and walks down the hall toward J.C. Penney.

"Where's he going?" my daughter asks in a panic.

"Santa's just going up on the roof to feed his reindeer," Jim explains.

"Looks like he's got to go to the bathroom from the way he's walking," my son speculates.

"Santa doesn't go to the bathroom," Amy says. "He's an elf."

What follows is a brief conversation (because I cut it off before anyone else in line can hear us) about whether Santa does or does not use the facilities.

The Big Man ambles back, admittedly looking a bit more comfortable, and at last, it's our turn for a visit.

That's when my 7-year-old pulls a fast one. "I want a hamster," she says. I look at Santa with a pained expression and shake my head, "no."

Picking up on my message, he says, "Are you sure?"

"OK, not a hamster – a new puppy. Ours is 4 years old already – he's not new anymore," she reasons

I shoot Santa a look that says, "Forget it."

She quickly slips in a request for a Barbie Town House before saying "cheese" for the camera. Before we know it, we're wandering the mall, holding tight to our overpriced 5x7 photo.

Santa didn't bring a puppy – and he certainly did not bring a hamster. (I'm already paying someone to eradicate rodents from my home. Why would I buy one and feed it?)

Santa didn't bring the Barbie Town House, either. Barbie shares the town house with her My Scene contemporaries. Their home is furnished with miniature designer furniture.

Why didn't Santa fulfill this request? Probably because he knows my daughter got an "Ear Piercing Barbie" for her birthday a few months ago, and he's aware we still hear the sound of Barbie's little metal earrings as they crackle their way up the hose of the vacuum cleaner every time we clean the house.

Santa also didn't bring the Usher CD my son wanted. Santa knows a lot about boys and girls who are naughty, but Usher writes lyrics about them. Santa just couldn't imagine a fifth-grade boy singing Usher's *Bad Girl:*

"I'm ready to be bad

I need a bad girl (Say 'yeah')

Get at me bad girl

What sexy lady's comin' home with me tonight?"

Santa didn't bring any video games with "mature" ratings ("there's nothing bad in them – they're just violent"), nor did he pack in his sack the DVD collector's edition of *Bridget Jones' Diary,* Prada accessories or concert tickets.

And yet, it wasn't disappointing at all.

Opening each gift, my children realized once again that Santa has an uncanny sense of what to choose. His presents aren't suggested by ad campaigns but by the intimate way he knows each child's heart.

Most of all, Santa brought our family a day to rediscover the magical power of generosity. Giving to each other transforms us into grateful beings, aware that we are blessed by the love we share and more importantly, by the promise of this holy season.

Thankfully, Christmas has just begun.

Must we have this dance?

The first thing I want to know when see my daughter's outfit is just where she thinks she's going dressed like this. So I say, "Just where do you think you're going dressed like this?"

"The dance," she says.

"What dance?" I ask.

"I told you, tonight is the middle-school dance," she answers, with just a bit too much emphasis on the word "told."

"No, you didn't," I decree.

What follows is a volley about a conversation I don't recall in which I supposedly granted permission to attend a dance about which I'm just now learning. As adolescents do, she characterizes comments made in passing as actual discussions about plans for the future.

I do lecture number 527 on "Organizing Plans in Advance," then get her to arrange the logistics for the evening. "Call a friend to join a carpool."

Then we move on to the wardrobe issue.

"The scooter skirt would be great in July, but since this is late September, why not put on some jeans instead? You might be more comfortable." I'm trying to make this sound like a suggestion, but we both know it's not.

We haggle a bit more about the sweater (black and a little severe) and flip-flops (dirty and too beatnik for my taste). At last, she appears wearing khakis and her new poncho, with her hair neatly brushed and some leather sandals. Appropriately attired, it's off to the dance with a small group of girlfriends.

I'm ambivalent about middle-school dances. Seems like the concept feeds all the age-appropriate insecurities children feel as puberty morphs them into adults. Most middle schoolers are locked in half-baked bodies, with the exception of the few alpha males who started shaving in sixth grade, and their female counterparts whose "womanly features" have fully taken shape.

In middle school, the disparity in physical development is surpassed only by the chasm in emotional maturity. Half of the youngsters want to dance and the other half look like they would rather have their braces tightened than move their feet to the music. This half would be the boys.

But at our school, the seventh- and eighth-grade dance is a rite of passage, so all the children go. Dressed in their coolest clothes, they line the walls of a darkened gymnasium. Either that or they run to the bathroom in clumps of four or six to assess who's "going out." When it's over, they breathe a collective sigh of relief they can go home and stop doing grown up things, like dancing.

On the upside, our middle school dance is highly regulated and well supervised – a benign event designed to build social skills.

Then again, what passes for dancing these days is not necessarily benign. This summer, we took our children to the county fair for a dose of country music, midway rides and a look at the prize-winning pigs. We're having good clean fun as we wander around eating snacks when suddenly we stumble into the "Teen Dance" area.

In fact, this is just a bunch of 13- to 15-year-olds, gathered around a picnic table on which rests the world's loudest boom box. It sends vibrations through the air as it drowns out the vintage rock-and-roll offered up by the midway operators.

All the boys in this crowd wear baggy shorts revealing the business end of their boxers, while the girls sport low-slung jeans with a hint of under-things peeking above the beltline and cropped t-tops. Tattoos and pierced navels abound.

If the attire doesn't tell us we've found "the fast crowd" among the Future Farmers of America, the dancing does. The entertainment industry has ratings for moves like these – letters you find deep into the alphabet.

Sandwiched in groups of three, they gyrate to a pulsating rap song, in what might have been, in ancient cultures, a communal fertility ceremony. In our culture, this is called "freak dancing."

My mouth drops open. All 12 of our feet stop dead in our tracks. My little one yells, "Shield your eyes" – her standard warning for kissing on television.

"Quick – let's ride the Matterhorn," I command as I redirect their stares away from the obscene display. Who cares if we spend another $20 in midway ride tickets? We need a diversion. Right now.

We swiftly move away from the "Teen Dance" area, processing what we've just seen. At only 6-years-old, my littlest daughter knows this was naughty. My son thinks it's just gross – but at age 10, he can't understand why those boys would hang out with girls in the first place when there's mud and barns full of pigs everywhere.

My older girls are bothered. They know teens behave this way, but seeing it makes them uncomfortable. This tasteless exhibition forces them to confront a culture we work hard to avoid.

Jim and I wonder aloud if this is what their parents had in mind when they sent their teens to the dance at the county fair. All we can do is shake our heads.

When we get to the Matterhorn, I decide to sit out the ride to watch my family from a nearby bench. Every time they pass me, they scream and squeal with laughter. No thumping drumbeat, no gritty lyrics, just the sweet sound of innocence floating through a summer sky.

Marybeth Hicks

Dear diary...
Mom was tacky
again today

*Dear Diary,
Words cannot express my most deepest
my most personal my most heartfelt feelings
that I just posted on my blog.
P.S. my sister is a little snoop!!*

"**W**here did you get that?" my eighth-grader demands to know. She looks accusingly at her little sister, who holds in her hand a tiny, green padlock shaped like a frog.

"I found it," comes the reply. "In the garage," she adds, a detail intended to lend credibility to her story.

"That's the lock to my diary. Give it back," Betsy commands.

"You don't even keep a diary," I reason with her, "and Amy's had the lock for two weeks, so obviously it's not something you really need." Betsy relents and lets her little sister keep the frog.

"The key is lost anyway," she concedes, "and besides, I hate diaries. Whenever I go back and read what I wrote, it's too embarrassing."

She has a point, and the reason I know this is – get ready for a true confession – I sometimes read her diary when she bothers to keep one, which is sporadic at best.

But before I'm accused of being the worst kind of parental snoop, let me just say that when a diary is pink and covered with pictures of purple unicorns, it's not likely to contain much by way of deeply personal expressions of "tween" angst.

More likely, it says things like, "I want to be Mrs. Orlando Bloom" and "I got my first zit today." I don't read diaries to get information; I read them for the entertainment value (OK, so I am the worst kind of parental snoop).

Around our house, diaries cause trouble. That's because I'm not the only one reading a journal that doesn't belong to me.

Years ago, my eldest daughter wrote in a diary about her frustration at having to share a room with her younger sister. Only she didn't just object to sharing living quarters, she objected to sharing airspace and occupancy on planet Earth. In short, she wrote a lot of mean and nasty stuff about her sibling, which caused some heartache when read by the subject of this private tirade.

This presented a tough parenting dilemma.

Betsy had no business reading a diary that didn't belong to her. Then again, Katie wrote some pretty spiteful things about her sister. It's not that she wasn't entitled to her feelings, but some thoughts probably are best left unexpressed.

So I did what any mother would do in a situation like this: I made them both feel guilty. Betsy got busted for snooping, Katie for sniping. I ripped the offending pages out of the book and said something about starving children in Third World countries (a Catholic mother's go-to line of defense, regardless of the issue at hand).

After that, diaries lost their appeal.

Monitoring the contents of a diary is a lot more complicated these days. The new "dear diary" is an online journal kept on "social networking" a site such as Myspace.com. This trend possibly reflecting the trend in our culture toward emotional exhibitionism.

If you can't tell your innermost thoughts to a studio audience on the *Jerry Springer Show* at least you can blog them for thousands of unknown readers on the World Wide Web.

A news story about teen blogs posed the question: Is it appropriate for parents to read their teenager's online journal or do a secret check for a Myspace.com page? The article said this was a "gray area" because "reading a teen's online blog might intrude on his privacy," jeopardizing the parent/child relationship.

I had to reread that part of the article a couple of times because it used the words "online blog" and "privacy" in the same sentence, which I found confusing.

An expert, Professor Paul Attewell from the City University of New York, actually said – and I'm not making this up – that reading your child's blog is "tacky and reprehensible." The article substantiated his credentials by stating he was funded by the National Science Foundation to research teens and technology.

Thank goodness, Prof. Attewell was not funded to research parenting.

Now, I don't want to overstate this, so I'll just say, comments like this professor's are what's wrong with America today.

First, "tacky and reprehensible" is when you walk into the high school cafeteria wearing sweats and smelling like toilet bowl cleaner to drop off the lunch your teen forgot, and you make a big fuss over it in front of her friends.

It's also "tacky and reprehensible" to sing with the radio when her friends are in the car, talk about guys you dated in high school, or suggest a hairstyle for her.

What isn't tacky or reprehensible is being a responsible parent. This means making it your business to know if your child is blogging and deciding whether this is acceptable to you.

If you allow blogging, it means setting standards so your child knows what is appropriate to post in cyberspace. And most of all, it means eliminating any expectation of privacy if your teen chooses to share personal thoughts and feelings with the cyber world.

So-called experts like Prof. Attewell aren't doing teens any favors, either. In our culture, too many parents behave like buddies to their children and not authority figures. His advice gives adults a permission slip to skip out on the hard work it takes to be aware of and involved in their teenager's lives.

The National Science Foundation isn't funding me for anything, so I guess I'm not an expert. Nonetheless, when it comes to parenting, I'm willing to be "tacky and reprehensible" if that's what it takes to do the job.

Marybeth Hicks

Fashion trends from the inside out

They were only 7 and 5 when my daughters learned what it meant to be a tramp. My mother told them.

It was our first "girls' getaway" – a weekend of intergenerational bonding over nail polish and a trip to the shopping mall. I had packed a few fashion magazines and a copy of *People* – the annual best- and worst-dressed edition – to peruse during the four-hour drive.

I did the driving, so my mother did the perusing. She perched her bright red reading glasses on the end of her nose and opened the slick pages of *People* to take in the full-color photos. On page after page, the magazine offered its take on celebrity-style statements – the daring, the delightful, the dazzling and the disastrous dresses that turned heads on red carpets from New York to Los Angeles and beyond.

My mom isn't one to hold back when she feels strongly about something. Suffice to say, the pages of *People* generated a visceral response as she expertly licked her fingers and flipped the flimsy paper of the special double issue.

"Look at this woman," she shrieked, holding up the magazine so I could glance over and see the photo without endangering us or the other folks on the expressway. "What a tramp."

"What's a tramp?" my younger daughter asked.

"A tramp is someone who dresses like this," my mom said in a roundabout explanation, slapping the photo for effect. "She's practically naked."

"Icks-nay on the amp-tray," I said in pig Latin. "We've never actually defined that term at home."

"Well, it's never too soon to know what a tramp is and how to avoid dressing like one," my mother declared.

That's the weekend my girls learned my mother's definition of "tacky" and what modesty means. At an early age, they understood that their clothing choices can tell the world who they are and what they stand for.

I've read modesty is making a fashion comeback, but you wouldn't know it by looking at what's on the racks for spring and summer. Paper-thin fabrics, belly-baring halter tops with sayings like "Ready or Not" and "Wild Child," skirts slit to here, animal prints – all designed to exude hypersexuality.

These are just the choices in the girls' department. The attire in the juniors' department is so explicit it belongs in a catalog with a heavy brown paper wrapper.

Apparently the folks on Seventh Avenue haven't heard about the modesty trend. They are not concerned about maintaining a wholesome, youthful image for today's young teens through the clothing they produce. In their relentless pursuit of "fashion" (a word that here means "money"), they offer season after season of tacky togs intended to cover little of the human anatomy.

It sometimes seems the skimpier the outfit, the higher the price tag.

In addition to promoting a heightened and inappropriate image of sexuality in young girls, the folks who make these clothes create an added burden for mothers everywhere – enforcing standards of decency for our daughters.

As if parents don't have enough to haggle over (boys, cars, curfews, homework, the volume on headphones, the importance of breakfast, the capacity of a laundry hamper), now we must explain why it's inappropriate to expose one's torso to a waiting world.

And not just the torso, but the panties that can't help but land slightly above the waistline of the jeans and the bra straps that can't be concealed because the spaghetti straps on the "cami" are just strings.

So far, I have managed to avoid dressing-room debates about these style trends, thanks to my mother's long-ago lesson about what it means to be "tacky" and how to avoid it.

But mothers of daughters can only do so much. Our struggle to send our girls into the world appropriately attired would be easier if we had support from mothers of teenage sons, like my girlfriend.

With four strapping boys in her home, she often has admiring girls hanging around. She likes it when the teenagers gather at her house because she can keep tabs on them, but she has rules, and one of those has to do with attire.

Once, when a friend of her high schooler's showed up scantily clad in short shorts and a shirt that barely covered her chest, my friend said to her, "Honey, you're welcome at my house, but you need to go home and put some clothes on. You may not visit my home dressed like this."

OK, so her boys didn't speak to her for two weeks. They got over it, and when they did, they learned that their mother expects them to treat women with dignity and respect even if a woman doesn't extend dignity or respect to herself.

It's no wonder teens struggle with decisions about expressing their sexuality when they're confronted with a daily dose of temptation. After all, what's a boy supposed to think when a girl comes to school in a T-shirt that reads "Hottie" across the front? Boys can only assume – justifiably – that she's not a walking thermometer but a girl on a mission.

Our girls can send an even bolder message than those printed on today's T-shirts – a message about self-esteem, self-respect and sexuality: It's not what's outside, but what's on the inside that matters most.

Our culture needs to rediscover an old but effective fashion trend: Leaving something to the imagination.

Marybeth Hicks

We get our "bling" at the orthodontist

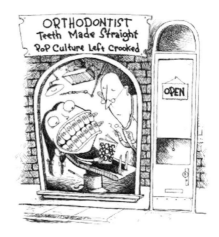

J ust when I think we've done a great job protecting our daughter from the influences of popular culture, there she sits in the orthodontist's office, reading *Seventeen Magazine*.

Is she wondering if she needs a therapist? There's a quick quiz to determine if she's really at risk or just needs to "talk to her parents or a trusted friend."

Does she want ideas to take a micro-mini skirt from daytime to evening? There are fashion suggestions to go from great to "glam" – most of which involve layers of "bling," although if my daughter ever appeared in one of these outfits, she couldn't leave our house.

Naturally, there are beauty tips to get the best hair ever, the best lips ever, the best eyebrows ever and even how to hide the bags under your eyes when you pull an all-nighter, presumably studying.

My daughter and I leaf through the publications piled on the coffee table as we wait for her appointment. Turns out, in addition to straight teeth, our orthodontist offers a crash course in pop culture for teens, with subscriptions to *YM*, *Teen People* and *J-14*.

The cover of *YM* (which used to stand for "young miss" but now means "your magazine") boasts several interesting features: "The hottest guys on the planet," "40 [expletive deleted] party looks" and "I got a boob job – two girls share the gross details." In case readers aren't convinced the details are gross, there's a photo inside taken mid-surgery of a girl's breasts, one side completed, the other waiting for the knife.

Teen People has the perennially smiling Hilary Duff on the cover – the favorite star of my 7-year-old. Inside, readers learn Hilary loves to shop, especially at Henri Bendel, where she's photographed spending roughly the same amount of money I might pay to resurface my driveway. This issue also asks the burning question, "Does your ponytail holder fit your personality?"

My favorite is *J-14* – not because it's good, but because it's so bad it reminds me why we put parental controls on everything in our home except the toaster.

J-14 – just for teens – offers "Hot stories about the 14 hottest stars" and a cover photo montage of Eminem ("the real reason" he "got naked"), Beyonce (her "shocking baby news") and Ashlee Simpson (why she "can't find love" – though her notorious embarrassing foray into late-night television might explain it).

I flip pages on my quest to read the *J-14* investigative report, "When gossip hurts" (advertised over a photo of Mary Kate Olsen), but the first thing I notice when I open the cover is the advertising.

Bubble-gum-flavored lipstick? A board game called "Mall Madness"? The holiday edition *Bratz* doll? An ad for Nickelodeon DVDs confirms the truth: I hold in my hand the battle plan for today's culture war.

Clearly, the objective is to indoctrinate children as early as possible into the permissive, materialistic mind-set that permeates these pages.

There in my orthodontist's office, readily available for children and young teens to pass the time while waiting to have their orthodontic hardware adjusted, is all the information they need to be culturally tuned-in. Articles about dating, sex (casually referred to as "hooking up"), and pregnancy fill the pages under headlines like "Boys, boys, boys" and "Could he be the one?"

What's most confusing are the mixed messages these publications send (although the slang is also baffling, and learning it is one reason I read the magazine while my daughter gets new brackets for her rubber bands).

On the one hand, it looks like they want to promote self-confidence, compassion and examples of real courage. Every issue has some feature that seems to say, "You're more than just your looks." One magazine highlights a girl's difficult recovery from an accident; another has a story on a teen's philanthropic efforts.

Yet these articles are contrived at best. They're sandwiched between pages of suggestive ads and regular features on "most embarrassing moments" – which almost exclusively have to do with clumsy intimate encounters.

The real reason to read these magazines is to learn how to "get your crush to notice you." They use the word "hot" on virtually every page because this is the goal – to be hot, look hot and date a hot guy. The sexually driven objectives of hair, make-up and fashion are obvious.

In fact, *Seventeen's* health section carries "the hook-up report," findings of a sex survey offering insights about teens' attitudes and beliefs, as well as explicit information about their sexual behaviors. Statistics about sexually transmitted diseases are the likely justification for the article.

What's worse, it's all packaged in cool, colorful graphics that appeal to girls as young as 8 and 9. Is this who's reading "the hook-up" report?

Perhaps the scariest proof these glossy books represent a battle for our daughters' minds and hearts is the editor's letter in which one publication describes itself not as a magazine, but as "your advisers. We work for you. And so we spend every single day trying to figure out, 'What should Our Girl know about now?'"

Unfortunately, there are too many things in this magazine that my 13-year-old daughter doesn't need to know, or even wonder about, yet.

I don't want her to be ignorant – on the contrary. I just want her to enjoy her innocence while she learns what it really means to become a woman in today's culture. That, and to have straight teeth.

Marybeth Hicks

Nobody warned me about driver's ed

Marybeth Hicks

Nobody warned me about driver's ed

Gently, at first, and then with considerable pressure, her foot presses down and she eases out of the warm, dark space that held her safe until this moment. Little by little, her toes dig and prod until an unexpected burst of energy catapults her into the waiting sunlight.

The van is out of the garage, and my first new driver is born.

We inch ever closer to the basketball hoop across the driveway and onto the adjacent strip of grass when she simultaneously lurches the van backward and forward, shifting from reverse to drive with a "glug." Not something I've heard before. This can't be good for my transmission.

"You need to come to a complete stop before you change gears, honey," I remind her kindly.

"Oh. Right. Sorry."

Nobody can quite prepare you for the moment when you hand your teenager the keys to a two-ton vehicular monster, lock yourself in its passenger seat, and entrust your very life to a person whose on-road driving instruction is measured in mere minutes – 360 minutes to be exact.

After just 24 classroom hours and six hours behind the wheel with her instructor, the unflappable "Mr. R.," my daughter Katie holds a learner's permit entitling – no, requiring – her to slide into the driver's seat and take years off my potential life expectancy.

But look around. Every driver in every big city and small town from Maine to Modesto had a parent who took them out to practice, all the while pressing hard on the floor mat in a fruitless effort to stop the car before making contact with a mailbox or a tree or the Lexus in front of them. If they could do this, so can I.

So here we are, on our way to the grocery store.

Katie spent the morning digging through kitchen cupboards in an effort to find something we desperately need and an excuse to drive me shopping.

I resisted, but it turns out we actually do need milk, bread and something for dinner. She grabs the keys and after a lengthy readjustment of seat, mirrors and air vents, we're under way.

Immediately, it's clear Mr. R. didn't teach "how to turn the car from one road to another." Funny, seems like he might have covered this. But each time we reach a corner, Katie puts on the turn signal and slows appropriately, only to die out in the middle of the turn.

"You need to give it some gas as you're coming out of the turn," I say.

"Oh. Right. Sorry."

At the next corner, we sputter again. "No really, honey, you need to give it some gas. If you don't, we're going to be hit from behind because the drivers in back of you think when you start to make a turn, you're actually going to complete it."

"Oh. Right. Sorry."

But on the main road, we're faced with yet another turn. I start thinking about where we could shop that wouldn't require us to alter the direction of the car. Again, the signal. Again, the brakes. Again, no gas.

Fear of the accident I described with extraordinary accuracy at the last corner overtakes me. This time I shout, "Go go go go go go go go!"

The combination of panic and repetition seems to have done the trick and she puts her foot down hard. We jump out of the turn and up a hill until I shout, "Slow down, slow down, slow down, slow down."

Self-preservation is the greatest teacher.

In some families, training new drivers is Dad's job. So far, in our household, this isn't the case. For one thing, my husband drives a stick shift, and while he professes a strong belief she should learn to use one for her own good ("What if there's an emergency and the only car at home is mine?"), there doesn't seem to be any urgency to get her over to the church parking lot and practice changing gears.

But there's also the language barrier. Men say things like "check your tachometer" and "reduce the degree of torque" instead of screaming, "Pick a lane!" and "Stop stop stop stop stop!"

We make it to the grocery store, get our food and head back in the van for the drive home. Incredibly, she's making progress on the turns, which now are uninterrupted, if not smooth, and I praise her improvement. "You're doing great," I tell her, and I mean it.

We don't talk much on the return trip. It's probably not a good idea to pick at every little thing while she's still getting used to the feel of the car, the curve of the road. Besides, I'm busy wondering how she went from eating my car keys in the grocery store to driving me there.

The year we have ahead to practice driving will fly by like the 15 years that brought us to this point. Before I know it, Katie will be behind the wheel of her own car, choosing its direction and setting it on a course of her own design.

Who knew in order to teach her to leave me, I'd have to trust her with my life?

Then again, why not? She's always trusted me with hers.

Marybeth Hicks

Date for our daughter or dead duck?

My husband loves to tell a story about his buddy, Dave. Dave's daughter had a date with a new boy. When the young man arrived, Dave greeted him at the door. "I'm working on something in the kitchen," he said. "Come on in."

The boy followed Dave, only to discover that he was in the midst of cleaning his shotgun.

Being an avid outdoorsman – not to mention the father of three girls – Jim appreciates the not-so-subtle message in his buddy's welcoming gesture.

In fact, Jim promises our daughters he'll be similarly occupied when some brave boy rings our doorbell. Usually, his fantasy of intimidation generates sighs and eye rolling.

Or this: "That's great Dad. Threaten the first guy who finally asks me on a date."

Our girls just don't understand how hard it is to be a dad to a daughter.

On the one hand, dads of daughters feel immeasurable pride in the lovely, talented young women growing up under their roofs.

On the other hand, dads know what boys have in mind.

Recalling the lewd and lascivious ideas that occupied their own thoughts when they were teens, they can't bear the notion that their innocent, unspoiled girls might play the starring role in some boy's dream of romance.

In my husband's case, the idea that our daughters will one day end up in the arms of some undeserving boys makes his face scrunch up in painful horror.

Of course, as our girls often remind Jim, this isn't something he needs to worry about yet.

It's not that they wouldn't enjoy being asked to school dances, movies or casual restaurant dinners. It's that high school dating – in the manner my husband fears – doesn't happen much anymore.

I'm convinced the last time a boy actually called a girl on her home phone and, with voice cracking and palms sweating, invited her to a school dance, was in the 1973 classic movie *American Graffiti*.

What does happen is this:

A school dance is announced, and right away, the guys and gals who already are "coupled" make plans to go together. (Even though this is something they obviously will do, an elaborate asking scenario is required, involving surprises left in lockers and announcements made in public.)

In the few weeks leading up to the dance, the "single" crowd starts jockeying for position. (Note: Single used to refer to people who were unmarried. Hollywood has redefined it to mean "romantically unattached.")

The process of pairing off needs encouragement, so girls make their preferences known, sending signals by telling a few key people – the ones everyone knows can't keep a secret. Naturally, these revelations always are preceded with the words, "You can't tell anyone ..." Yeah, right.

The boys are supposed to hear these rumors and act on them. Under the current dating mores (if you can call them mores) it's considered rude to ask a girl to a dance who doesn't already want to go with you.

Huh?

In the end, there are couples who go to dances as "couples" and some who go as "friends." (What else would you be?) Then there are couples who go to dances as "friends" and end up as "couples" by the end of the evening – elevating their relationships to the status of "going out."

Of course, there's a whole subset of couples who go to school dances: the ones generated by girls who don't wait to be asked but instead take matters into their own hands.

In our post-feminist culture, the rules about who asks whom to a dance are irrelevant because anyone is free to do the asking. Girls who ask boys to dances run the risk of being labeled as "spoilers," though, because they aren't necessarily in the loop on the whole "sending-out-signals" thing.

In fact, there aren't any rules anymore about dating. Traditional assumptions about who makes the plans, who drives and who pays for the outing are as outdated as the notion that you need a date for a dance in the first place.

You don't. You can just go with a group of friends.

Confused yet?

It gets more complicated. Teens today wouldn't go on a "date" as we adults know it. This is because dating is something you do with someone with whom you're already "going out."

Let's review: You don't go on a "date" unless you're "going out" with someone, and you don't "go out" with someone you're not "dating."

Chicken? Egg? Anyone?

In an effort to get a better handle on high school dating, I even did an Internet search. I figured there must be some new rules for the current generation of teens. Sadly, the responses I got on a search for "teens and dating" almost all dealt with sex.

No wonder Jim's face contorts at the thought of our teenage girls going out on a date.

Suffice to say because our daughters are "single," my husband doesn't have to make any immediate plans for his shotgun other than the deft and determined killing of waterfowl.

Then again, when the opportunity finally presents itself to open our front door to a young man whose intention it is to spend an evening with one of our girls, that boy had better be prepared to talk hunting – or be hunted.

Marybeth Hicks

And now, the line in the sand

I t's been happening since fall, so I guess I shouldn't be surprised. First, his clothes looked as if they had been made for someone else – someone with shorter arms and legs. The school pants I bought at the start of sixth grade fit like clam diggers by Christmas. In February, I ripped out the hems and told my son to ignore the little threads hanging down on his sneakers.

That tactic got us through the winter until the school dress code allowed shorts again, but it didn't solve the sleeve-length issue on his uniform shirt. He looks like Frankenstein, but don't tell him.

Come to think of it, his sneakers were too snug just weeks after they were purchased. Jimmy lobbied for new ones for a couple of months, but I put him off on the grounds he was in a growth spurt and buying new shoes would be a waste of money.

When I finally had his feet measured at the shoe store, I discovered we had skipped two full sizes between purchases. Oops.

The next thing I knew, Jimmy announced he was growing out his hair. In my mind, this was his official proclamation that he is donning the mantle of the preteen. In no time, I expect he will give up bathing and the transformation will be complete.

With all the physical symptoms in evidence, I guess this week's conversation in the van between my son and his buddies should not have shocked me.

In the span of one short drive from our neighborhood to the gym where the boys had basketball practice, Jimmy and his pals discussed: girls, Jon's new instant-messaging buddy list, girls, the underarm hair on the guy from last summer's basketball league, a classmate's obsession with online computer games, girls and food.

Mind you, we were in the van for all of seven minutes. They didn't discuss these topics so much as mention them, giggle, mention something else, giggle, roll their eyes, giggle, and then I think someone burped. Such is the discourse of the sixth-grade male.

Sixth grade ends in five days, and that can mean only one thing: Seventh grade is coming, and it's time for me to draw the line in the sand.

On one side: the "culture of cool," a media-saturated, consumer-driven state of pseudo-adulthood in which otherwise sweet children are sucked in and corrupted by the vacuum of pop-culture values, graphically depicted on MTV.

On the other side: "geekdom," a place where childhood innocence is preserved and protected and children are (happily) uncool enjoying oddball pastimes such as reading, chess and playing outdoors while living under the banner of "late bloomer."

Figuratively, that line represents the barrier between us and a culture that would steal our son's boyhood and replace it with cynicism and worldliness gained not from life experience, but from experiencing life through the media.

Practically, it's the standard that will dictate Jimmy's social status for the next two years of middle school. While many of his peers will have access to the "culture of cool," we'll be making choices that limit the development of our son's social savvy.

PG-13 movies?

Unlimited access to the Internet?

A personal music download account?

A bedroom TV?

In a word: No. In a phrase: No.

It won't be easy to hold that line; it's a struggle we've experienced already while fighting to maintain a wholesome environment for our two older daughters. There seems to be no end of potential threats to childhood innocence, no limit to how low the culture will stoop to spread its twisted notion of what's cool.

Just this week, our school counselor sent home a letter warning parents to be on the lookout for new and dangerous trends, such as "The Choking Game" (in which players asphyxiate themselves in pursuit of an "oxygen high") and the blog site www.myspace.com, the Internet craze that promotes self-expression to the point of risky self-exposure. The counselor's letter also included a laundry list of "stressors" that adolescents might be feeling, from pressure to succeed in school to concerns about family finances.

The letter was good. It spoke directly to parents about things we need to understand, and it offered suggestions for talking to our children and keeping the lines of communication open.

Nevertheless, it made me sad that my young son is growing up in a world where children aren't sheltered but instead must be educated about things that insidiously threaten their well-being.

As much as I wanted to slip that letter under a stack of papers on my desk and keep Jimmy from knowing about its content, I knew the issues were too close to home to avoid. Seventh grade is just around the corner, after all.

So I talked to Jimmy while he ate a bowl of ice cream. I described the letter and asked him if he had any questions. I reassured him that he could always talk to his dad and me when he hears about things he doesn't understand.

When it was clear he wasn't going to participate in a dialogue, I tousled his new longer hair and said, "Why is it when we have these talks you seem so uncomfortable?"

Jimmy sighed and said, "Mom, I just want to be a kid.

"Who could blame you?" I said. "Be a kid."

Then again, with that kind of wisdom, it's clear he's growing up already.

Seeing clearly makes daughter "emo"

As if there weren't enough reasons for insecurity and teenage angst when you're a high school freshman, my 14-year-old daughter was told recently that she needs glasses.

Not long ago, Betsy started complaining of headaches at school and an inability to see the chalkboard clearly, so I took her to the optometrist, and sure enough, she is nearsighted.

It's not the first time we've had her eyes checked. A few years ago, during basketball season, her formerly reliable jump shot started flying wildly all over the gym – most often above the top of the backboard – and it was a shot she took with unfortunate frequency.

I thought she might have a depth-perception problem, but a visit to the eye doctor confirmed she had 20/20 vision, a discovery that prompted her brother to say, "I told you, Mom. She just stinks."

Be that as it may.

This time around, the diagnosis is clear – or should I say, fuzzy? – so we find ourselves engaged in the delicate task of redefining Betsy's appearance with prescription eyewear.

Choosing glasses is a complex decision, in part because eyewear seems to make a statement about personality. One style suggests, "I'm practical and not a risk taker," while another frame might say, "I'm desperate for attention – do I have yours?" The trick is to find a frame that subtly speaks for you without accentuating your uneven eyebrows – or your nose.

Choosing glasses puts a whole lot of focus on your nose, magnifying faults in ways you've never suspected.

Right away I rule out anything with a designer name on the stem, for which I would pay an additional $100.

She doesn't balk because she knows I could limit her choice to a sensible tortoise-shell frame that would stand up to teenage abuse, and so far I haven't stipulated durability over design.

We spend at least an hour sorting through the racks of sample frames. One is "too John Lennon." Another is "too Lucille Ball." When I say the red ones are "too Sally Jessy Raphael" I have to spend five minutes explaining who the talk-show hostess is.

Eventually, we realize we keep pulling the same frame off its plastic "face" and putting it on Betsy's. In the frame-selection process, this is how you know you're finished – you try the same glasses again and again until you discover the frame about which you register the fewest objections.

Betsy settles on rectangular lenses in a black frame, but not all black; the inside of the frame is a zippy shade of green, and the stems have green crisscross designs from tip to temple. We think they are smart and even a little bit cool.

But what do we know?

Monday comes, and Betsy heads off to school in her new specs, finally able to focus on the essential notes and cryptic squiggles on the board and also able to discern distant objects such as street signs and cute guys in the cafeteria (which she strenuously argues is not her goal).

The first school day in glasses comes to an end, and I'm curious to know what her friends think of her new look.

"They said my glasses were emo."

"What's emo?" I ask.

"I have no idea."

We head to the computer and get on www.urbandictionary.com, searching "emo" for a definition. Sure enough, there are thousands of entries, and there even are categories of ways in which you can be emo.

We find this definition:

"Genre of soft-core punk music that integrates unenthusiastic melodramatic 17-year-olds who don't smile; high-pitched overwrought lyrics and inaudible guitar riffs with tight wool sweaters; tighter jeans; itchy scarves (even in the summer); ripped chucks with favorite band's signature; black-square-rimmed glasses; and ebony greasy, unwashed hair that is required to cover at least 3/5ths of the face at an angle."

This explains a lot. We also find this more succinct description:

"Like a Goth, only much less dark and much more Harry Potter."

We keep scrolling emo entries until we find a lengthy and informative explanation that says the term does not mean emotional, as most teens believe, but refers to "emotive hard-core," a music genre. The writer of this historical perspective notes that originally the term didn't have anything to do with categorizing an entire segment of adolescent America – the ones suburban moms like me might call "disaffected youths."

The part about the black eyeglass frames leaves Betsy a bit undone. "An emo kid is a depressed person who shops at Hot Topic in the mall," she says, referring to the national chain located in nearly every major shopping center where teens can buy scary-looking apparel.

(According to the urban dictionary, however, "emo kids" would claim to hate Hot Topic. They pride themselves on nonconformity, in a conformist sort of way.)

Not Betsy's style at all.

I'm sure as heck not going back to choose another pair of glasses in a different stereotypical style ("Would you rather be preppy?" I ask. She is horrified), so we start thinking of pithy comebacks the next time someone says her new glasses are emo.

"The next time," I suggest, "just ignore them and pretend you're writing an anguished poem about being misunderstood."

It's the emo thing to do.

Busting the "teenage monster myth"

My daughter and I made a promise to each other several years ago, and we're trying to keep it.

We swore we would avoid becoming the stereotypical mother and daughter through her teen years

We wouldn't subscribe to the myth that teenage girls naturally become disrespectful and condescending to their moms or that moms are unreasonable and oblivious to the real feelings of their girls.

Mind you, this is a cultural myth that has a whole lot of traction keeping it going. Just stand outside the fitting room in any Gap store on a weekend and listen to an entire generation of girls treat their mothers with the same courtesy and respect they would afford a cockroach (the same mothers whose credit cards are relied on at the checkout counter). You'll know why society takes for granted the truth of the "difficult teen."

Back when Katie's 13th birthday approached, I heard endless warnings about what my future would hold with a teenager in my home. Because she is my oldest, I had no experience with teens, so parents offered the conventional wisdom.

"Just wait," I was told. "She'll turn into a monster."

Or this encouraging thought: "Get ready to find out just how stupid you are."

And my favorite piece of optimistic advice: "Don't worry. It'll get better by the time she's 23."

If I had a nickel for every time someone told me to get ready for the change in my daughter, I would have – well, I would have a big, honking pile of nickels.

I couldn't imagine or believe that my delightful teenager was destined to become a holy terror for 10 years or that there was nothing I could do about it. More than that, I wouldn't stipulate to an assumption I simply didn't buy.

Why should I accept that my daughter couldn't help but treat me like a necessary encumbrance or that I should wish away her growing years because of excessive obnoxiousness? Who says?

Not me. Not us.

Back then, on trips to the store or at school functions, Katie and I started to notice moms and daughters. We saw many whose relationships we admired, but sadly, it was easier to spot examples of the kind of behavior we wanted to avoid.

Whenever we overheard daughters speaking disrespectfully or impatiently to their mothers, we talked about it – not only about the lack of courtesy on the part of the girl, but about the lack of self-respect in a grown woman who would let her child get away with a tone of voice that seemed to say, "Mom, you are an idiot, and you are embarrassing me."

I made sure to stress to Katie that the girl wasn't the only one at fault. After all, teens who talk back to their parents do this because they know they can. Apparently, parents who accept such communication are getting the behavior they pretty much expect.

Our observations brought Katie to the conclusion that she didn't want to sound like the girls who "dissed" their moms, and I concluded I wouldn't step into the role of maternal doormat.

That's when we made our deal. We would do it differently.

I would try to be patient and understand when stress, hormones, lack of sleep and general feelings of teenage discombobulation ran rampant through her growing mind and body.

She would remember that "Honor your parents" is on God's short list of important ideals for human behavior. It wasn't something she could choose to do or not do – it was a given.

To be clear, we were not agreeing to be "buddies." I love my teenager, but I'm not her friend; I'm her mother. Big difference. I insisted she treat me like a mother even if our relationship is mostly friendly.

Busting this myth would be a 50-50 bargain. Katie had to uphold her promise to speak respectfully, just as I had to expect and demand the behavior my role deserved.

We made that deal four years ago, before high school started – before we entered the world of cell phones and car keys and a growing sense of independence that clearly wants its way.

Still, most of the time we do all right.

Katie has a propensity to say "I know" with a bit more assertiveness than I would like. It's not so much "I know" as, "You have told me this same thing 110 times before, and I wish you would stop telling me." She manages to get all that in there by stretching out the word "know" into two long syllables.

I have a tendency to lecture rather than listen. OK, not a tendency. A habit.

So far, though, I've only had to remind her of our promise a few times.

Doing this is the one thing that jars her – in part because she treasures our relationship – but also because she's a girl who keeps her word, and when we set out to bust this myth, she intended to succeed.

Then again, what Katie doesn't know is she already has succeeded. Simply promising to be different made her different

In a world that makes excuses for disrespectful behavior on the grounds it's just a part of growing up, Katie is proving my contention that this is just a myth.

We still have a way to go, but so far, so good.

Marybeth Hicks

Game defines who we really are

"Let's play Desert Island," I said to Amy. "Pretend you are going to an uncharted island and you can take just three things with you. Go get the three things you would take along."

This is how I got rid of Amy so I could enjoy some adult conversation with my friend Sarah, who also happens to be Amy's former third-grade teacher.

Several minutes passed while Amy retreated to her room to find the three items that would define her existence on her remote island home. I wondered – though not aloud, so as not to appear neurotic – if one of her three things would be a toothbrush.

Amy reappeared a short time later, and here is what she brought: her teddy bear, the "All About Me" poster she made in first grade, and a novelty pen that plays famous quotes from the movie *Napoleon Dynamite* at the push of a button.

Sarah and I enjoyed Amy's explanations for choosing each of her items, then managed to get in another few minutes of conversation when I asked Amy to return her belongings to her room. By then, I think Amy had caught on to the real purpose behind my "game," so she left us alone for a while. (Moms are sneaky that way, but hey – sometimes we have to do whatever it takes to string together two sentences of adult conversation.)

If I were asked, I would have no problem choosing three items to define my life.

The first item would be an economy-size bottle of Tide with bleach alternative. I buy almost as many gallons of Tide in a week as I buy of milk. When I'm out of Tide, I feel oddly unsettled, as if my purpose in life is at risk of slipping into a mud-encrusted, sweat-infused pair of soccer socks. I wouldn't want to be stuck on an island without a meaningful purpose in life, and I realized long ago my purpose is laundry.

Don't roll your eyes when I say this, but my second item for the desert island would be my cell phone. (It's just a game, so the fact there would be no cell-phone service is irrelevant).

I honestly don't know how our mothers raised us without cell phones. In fact, it's hard to recall the days when my land line was attached to the wall of my kitchen, a 75-foot-spiral cord stretched across the room and out the sliding door to the back yard, where I talked on the phone from a lawn chair while watching toddlers in the sandbox.

Back then, I was emancipated by my cordless phone, which enabled me to load and unload the washing machine while talking to my sisters.

These days, I'm attached to my cell phone like an on-call physician or the CEO of a Fortune 500 company. I'm not that important, but tell that to a daughter who can't find her wallet or a son who calls to remind you to pick him up from basketball practice.

The final item I would choose? Post-It notes. Even on a desert island, I'm a mother juggling the lives of a busy family and an irresponsible dog. No further explanation is necessary.

The real fun in the Desert Island game is to see if you can predict the items your loved ones might choose. It's a way to assess how well you know someone.

For example, I'm sure my son Jimmy would choose a basketball, his LeBron James basketball shoes and his friend Jon. Come to think of it, his choices would mean life on a desert island would be the same as life here in our neighborhood.

My husband's items would be somewhat esoteric: A copy of the 2004 Baseball Encyclopedia, a bag of jawbreakers and a six-pack of dark beer. He would insist these items could assure his contentment; he accuses me of overpacking whenever we travel.

Of course, the things we choose don't really stand for who we are. Still, in our consumer-driven, materialistic world, it's easy to forget that all our stuff could be left behind – and in fact, some day will be left behind. I suppose that's what makes the game interesting – the idea that we could take just a few things with us that reflect what we're really all about

As well as I know my 8-year-old daughter, I wouldn't have predicted the three items Amy brought from her room to help demonstrate what she values, and yet they made perfect sense.

The poster shows photos of Amy from infancy through age 6 – the happy first years when memories merge into one undefined sense of childhood. She is smiling in every picture.

The teddy bear's well-worn fur reflects the loving grasp of Amy and all three of her older siblings, all of whom owned Teddy at one time. He stands for both security and family traditions.

The *Napoleon Dynamite* pen, well, it's just quirky. Not to mention, it makes her laugh, and we all need to laugh when we're stranded.

Then again, if we were all stuck on that desert island together, Amy could write a message with that silly pen on one of my Post-It notes and toss it into the ocean in one of her dad's empty beer bottles.

She'd probably get us rescued in the end.

Marybeth Hicks

A Silent Night for mother and son

When I climbed into bed, the sheets felt like thin strips of refrigeration. I pulled the comforter up to my ears and shivered as I waited for my body to generate enough heat to turn my toes from blue to toasty.

Now, at 3:35 in the morning, a wave of warmth rolls over me like an incoming tide and wakes me from my proverbial "long winter's nap."

Hot flash? Maybe. Let's not go there.

I cool myself down by hanging my feet outside the covers to let the heat escape through my sweaty soles. After a couple of moments, I'm aware that I'm not only hot but thirsty.

I resign myself to the inevitable. Sleepy as I am, I have to get out of bed.

I roll back the blankets and head to the kitchen for a drink of water.

Everything in the kitchen is just as I left it four hours ago, but in the wee hours, it's a peaceful space, not the busy, bustling place it is when all the lights are on.

It's so quiet I can hear the furnace running, though it doesn't run often at night since my husband turns it down to the "frigid" setting to save money.

I used to balk, but with energy costs such as they are, and my new propensity to overheat, I don't argue.

I take my water and wander from room to room. Yesterday's paper is strewn over a coffee table. One of the children must have been reading it since the sections are disassembled. There are pillows on the floor, along with the dog's chew toy and someone's shoes. It's not a mess, but it's lived in.

In the dining room, I stand in the window and look out over the snow-covered street. The yellow glow from the street lamps casts long shadows in our yard. Everyone else left their Christmas lights on. (Ours are off, of course. Did I mention my husband and the energy bill?)

The air outside is completely still, allowing tufts of snow to sit unmarred on the branches of the barren maple trees. There is snow between the needles of the fir tree next to our driveway. It's dangerously cold out there - the low is supposed to be something like 2 degrees - and I'm amazed that a night so brutal is also so beautiful.

Thinking about the temperature outside prompts me to go to Jimmy's room and make sure he hasn't kicked off his blanket. Since his bedroom is above the garage, it gets pretty cold, and what with the furnace running only occasionally, it won't get very warm anyway.

There's no nightlight in Jimmy's room – he's a "total darkness" sleeper. Even in the dark, I spot the hazards between his bedroom door and his sleeping form under the comforter. I walk around a Nerf ball, yesterday's sweatshirt and a pile of Legos and sit on the edge of his bed.

Jimmy is the soundest and easiest sleeper of all my children. I don't know if this is because he's a guy - which means he's hardwired to sleep anywhere, at any time – or because he expends so much energy throughout the day that his body simply shuts down when his head hits the pillow. He's the one child I must tuck in almost immediately or else the chance to say "goodnight" is lost in soundless slumber. Lucky boy.

I softly rub his cheek, knowing my movements won't disturb him. There's just enough light coming from the window to see his eyelids flutter back and forth, following the pattern of his unconscious thoughts as they speed through the deepest recesses of his mind.

There's something in this moment, profound in its silence, when all my son's dreams and hopes and wishes seem to reach out and grab my heart. His life is so incomplete, so unformed; it holds such promise and purpose yet to be discovered.

On this night - this "Silent Night" – I realize my thoughts and prayers for my son must be the very kinds of thoughts and prayers that every mother has for her boy.

Mothers of kings and soldiers, of presidents and scientists and artists and laborers, from age to age, wander the house in the stillness of a winter night and sit at the side of the bed.

We all think about the men our sons could become, should become.

So must Mary have sat by a sleeping Jesus, listening to him softly inhale and exhale, watching his eyes dance from side to side as images flashed across his perfect mind.

Did she wonder about his dreams? Did she pray they'd come to pass?

Did she pray he would be the man he was created to be?

Did she dare ask God to make him great? Or to let him change the world?

I realize in this moment that all these years I've been praying that God would grant my best hopes for Jimmy and his deepest desires for himself.

But I wonder if instead, Mary prayed that God would grant not her fondest hopes for her son, but his?

Perhaps she did.

Perhaps on those silent nights when she watched her son in peaceful slumber, she understood that even a mother's heart can't hold the infinite potential that exists only in the thoughts of God.

Marybeth Hicks

To tell the truth, kids don't

Exhibit A

T he morning rush comes to its usual chaotic peak as I begin the hunt for shoes.

We have a great system for storing shoes – oversized baskets, marked with the names of all four children, neatly stacked on shelves in the garage.

Theoretically, the shoes would go from their owners' feet into a corresponding basket. I stress "theoretically" here because in reality, the shoes pile up on the landing, impeding egress from our house.

In cold weather months, the system is complicated by two baskets of hats, gloves and scarves stored on the shelf above the shoes.

Conceptually, the children would wear the necessary accessories when the temperature warrants an extra layer, returning them to a communal storage basket when they get home – conceptually.

When I open the door to the garage to fetch my daughter's school shoes, there's a pile of mismatched mittens and two upended baskets of hats and scarves in a heap on the landing.

"Who dumped these baskets?" I shout. My voice echoes through the dark garage, bouncing back into the house.

Four voices answer in perfect unison, "Not me."

I might have known. "Not me" is the perpetrator of countless acts of mischief

"Look," I say in my strongest mom voice, "I'm not leaving this house until one of you admits to dumping this stuff all over the garage."

Amy quickly confesses, pleading guilty with an explanation: "I needed mittens and I couldn't reach the baskets and then they fell and I couldn't get them back on the shelf," she explains urgently.

Truth telling has its rewards around my house. Rather than scold her, I remind her to ask for help when she can't reach something and thank her for 'fessing up. Then we resume the morning mayhem and head out the door.

I'll never understand why children try to lie their way out of things. They're terrible liars.

Case in point: Last winter, I asked my son if he put the dog out to do his morning business. Jimmy said "yes," so it seemed odd the dog was scratching at the back door.

I opened the door to offer the pup a second chance, thinking maybe his little canine kidneys were working overtime, only to discover fresh, white snow covering the back steps. No dog tracks, no yellow evidence of doggy relief – only the obvious proof my son lied to my face.

Child-development experts reassure us that lying comes at age-appropriate intervals. First, children lie to get what they want. Later, they lie to stay out of trouble. Supposedly, they grow out of it.

Here's my problem with this theory: Some people don't grow out of it. As children, they lie to their teachers to avoid detention. Later, they lie to the grand jury to avoid incarceration. These people are called "liars" and they're everywhere.

Plus, I believe a 9-year-old who lies about something minor, like putting his dog out, will absolutely lie at 19 about where he was until 4 a.m. and why he smells like a Texas roadhouse.

This is why I make such a fuss when I ask Jimmy if he brushed his teeth. He says "yes," while layers of plaque encrust themselves to his otherwise pleasant smile.

Clearly, I have work to do on the importance of personal integrity, not to mention hygiene. I decide the next time he lies I'll respond more forcefully.

Soon enough, I catch him trying to sneak contraband into school – Sharpie permanent markers. When I confront him, he says he doesn't know where they came from.

The way I react, you'd think he's a regular villain on *Law and Order.*

I get a full-blown sermon going, my vocal chords inflamed, veins bulging out of my neck.

I tell him he's ruining his relationship with me because I can't trust him.

I tell him his deceitful behavior is getting to be a bad habit.

I tell him he's a lousy liar anyway, and he lies about things that are just plain stupid.

"Dumb and dishonest is no way to go through life," I conclude. OK, it's a little harsh, but if your mom won't be straight with you, who will?

He spends a whole day on the dark side of a mother's love. Not even an unsolicited offer to take out the garbage gets a smile out of me.

Later that night, I sit on the edge of his bed to tuck him in. Curled up under his quilt, he looks tiny, not like the gangly child who seems to grow a couple of inches every other day. I give him a hug and tell him it's because I love him that I'm committed to teaching him honesty.

He climbs out of bed and gets a piece of paper from his desk – a note he wrote earlier in the evening. "Dear Mom, I'm writing you this letter to say that I am very sorry that I lied to you ... I know it's important to be trustworthy." It's signed "your loving son."

This is progress.

We talk a little more in the dark, making our peace and promising the next day will be a new beginning. "Being an honest man is more important than anything you can become," I say to his silhouette.

"You're going to make a lot of mistakes in life – we all do. Just don't make the mistake of losing your integrity."

Marybeth Hicks

The awesome power of "it" girls

How was your day?" I ask as my daughter climbs into the van.

She lifts her backpack onto the seat next to her and clips her seat belt with a self-satisfied smile. "Great," Amy says enthusiastically. "One of the girls said I'm cool."

"Wow. How does she know?" I ask.

"Mom, that should be obvious," Amy says, implying my ignorance.

It isn't obvious, at least not to me.

She smiles and waves goodbye to a group of girls standing on the sidewalk and then settles back, crosses her legs and sits up tall in her seat. Clearly, she's feeling good about herself.

I change the subject, checking on the evening's homework assignments and confirming that she turned in the permission slip for an upcoming field trip. It's the typical conversation of a Tuesday afternoon.

In the back of my mind, though, I know today is more than just an average Tuesday. Today, a popular girl created the possibility that my daughter might be popular, too. Today, Amy felt accepted and appreciated. Today, her world seems, like, totally awesome.

Tomorrow, it will all be different.

Sure enough, not the next day, but a week later, the girl who told Amy she was cool has decided my daughter is, in fact, weird.

Because she's the alpha girl, her declaration is met with universal agreement and approval by the rest of the cool crowd. Suddenly, just as quickly as Amy's social status had risen, she returns to the rank of "outsider."

This Tuesday, when I pick her up after school, there are tears and trauma as Amy tries to understand the fickle nature of friendship.

She thinks maybe this is just a blip on the social screen – a recess gone bad; a misunderstanding.

She doesn't know why she's weird or why anyone would tell her such a thing even if she thought so, or why others who previously behaved like friends would believe it. She's confused.

I have been down this road with daughters two times before. I could see it coming. By third grade, the egalitarian atmosphere of kindergarten coalesces into well-established cliques that mandate who may sit together at lunch, who may swing on the swing set during recess, who is invited to after-school play dates and weekend sleepovers.

Sure enough, here I am again in third grade with a daughter who has just discovered there are "it" girls, and they have the power to decide whether she is one of them.

Kind and caring one day, caustic and cruel the next, "it" girls define who is cool (like them).

They're natural leaders, assembling an entourage of followers whose role it is to work at continually winning the "it" girls' approval. Of course, bestowing approval is what makes their role as "it" girls relevant, and thus, their favor changes from day to day – and often from math class to music.

This is why Amy was cool one week and weird the next.

"Why do they think I'm weird?" she wonders as I tuck her into bed. It's a question I anticipated, just as I expected she would soon discover the truth about her place in the social order.

"Well, here's the thing," I begin gently, "I don't think you're weird, but I think you're different. And some people think being different is weird."

What follows is the first of what I know will be countless conversations about why she doesn't fit in and how it feels to be excluded.

For now, she concludes it's because I won't buy clothes for her at Limited Too or let her have Bratz dolls or carry a purse to school. She's savvy enough to understand that certain rules apply to getting close to the "it" girls, some of which clearly are about owning the right stuff and showing it off.

Later, she'll realize it's more than that.

Later, she'll understand she is different because we're raising her to be different, a unique individual, free to explore her own interests, her own style and her own self-expression. She'll figure out that it was more important to us that she be herself than that she be like – or liked by – the "it" girls or anyone else.

Thankfully, I know this strategy will work. I expect Amy will learn one of these days, as her older sisters have discovered, that "it" girls are important only if you seek out their affirmation. As soon as you don't care anymore, you negate their significance. Of course, this was always possible, even if it seemed unthinkable back in third grade when you first experienced their awesome power.

Not that this is any comfort on a Tuesday night, with tears streaming down your tiny face.

In the yellow glow of her night light, she seems so small to me that I can't believe we're already here, in third grade, negotiating the rough waters of female friendship. And yet I know this is just the beginning.

Fortunately, I'm confident I can get her safely to shore on the other side. What I don't know is how to get her there without her heart breaking every so often along the way.

Marybeth Hicks

Driving through another rite of passage

"**S**o when you say the car has rust on it, what exactly do you mean?" Katie asked tentatively. I had already told her its moderate price tag ("moderate" here being a word that means "less than the cost of the new pots and pans I received last Christmas"), so she ought to have known the car is well-worn, at best.

"I mean rust. That orange stuff that collects when metal corrodes. But don't worry – it goes nicely with the color of the car," I said.

Apparently, this isn't what my teenage daughter expected when she learned we were purchasing a third family car that she may use to drive to school and elsewhere in her busy teenage life.

Note I didn't refer to the car "we were purchasing for her." Semantics are important here, at least to my husband and me. We're very careful to refer to this vehicle as the one we will make available to our daughter. It's not "her car."

"Her car" would be a vehicle for which she saved, shopped and committed financial resources. "Her car" would be registered in her name, insured by her and maintained by her. Contrary to theories of common law, possession in this case is unimportant. Just because you hold the keys doesn't mean the car is yours.

We bought the car because, after more than a year of driving on a learner's permit, our daughter finally will be a licensed driver this month. When that happens, we want the added convenience of another driver to ease the relentless transportation hassles associated with four busy children. We got the car for us, not for her.

That's why the car was not presented with a bow on the rearview mirror, or in any other way that would associate this purchase with Katie's 16th birthday – no designer key ring, no value-pack of car wash certificates, not even a gift-wrapped ice scraper. We're very careful to make it seem this car is a burden of sorts.

Nonetheless, the next thing she wanted to know about the car after she asked about the color was whether it has an in-dash CD player.

She's excited, and I can't blame her. In fact, I may be one of the few mothers in America who is as thrilled that her child is obtaining a driver's license as is the new driver.

For a while now, I've had a feeling reminiscent of the ninth month of pregnancy – the time when the duration of gestation surpasses the fear of childbirth. I know this is going to be painful, but I'll do pretty much anything to get this child out into the world. I look forward to her mobility much as I dreamed of walking without waddling during my 30s.

It's a rite of passage for us both. My daughter's new responsibilities as a driver will bring her the freedom she craves. She's excited to feel more grown up, more like the adult she is working hard to become. She envisions herself running her own errands, carrying a purse for good reason, even taking on new activities such as volunteer work or a part-time job.

This particular rite of passage is a challenge for me, however. It's not that I want to hold her back – on the contrary, I know she's ready and able to be out in the world, ferrying herself around town to and from school, sports practice and lessons. She's proved time and again that she appreciates the seriousness of getting behind the wheel of a car.

Still, I'm struggling with what I must give up to help her grow. Up to now, riding in the car is an extension of being at home together – it's a place she can burst into tears or quickly tell her big news. It holds secrets and hopes and plans shared in private.

When I hand over the keys to that rusty but reliable old car, I hand her the space to keep from opening her heart. I can't help but ask myself, when she no longer needs a ride, will she still need the driver?

It's a question we parents must quell in the interest of rearing secure, independent children. At some point, I have to trust that the hours spent talking and listening – in and out of the family car – have built a bond that no mere change in transportation can render obsolete.

I'm pretty sure my sentimentality will soon give way to the rediscovery of many precious hours formerly spent as a chauffeur. With fewer children needing my "kiddy cab" services, I may even have time to read books or walk the dog or take up knitting. Who knows?

Besides, if ever I miss the time spent chatting with my daughter while driving her around town, I can always insist on giving her a ride. After all, the car she's driving isn't really hers, anyway.

Marybeth Hicks

Nobody warned me about driver's ed

Marybeth Hicks

'The talk' is not a one-time event

Marybeth Hicks

'The talk' is not a one-time event

We sat together on the sofa, Katie's slight, 5-year-old frame tucked neatly next to me. She leaned in, draped her arm across my burgeoning belly and asked, "How is that baby going to get out of there?"

That moment 11 years ago is the one many parents dread, but I was prepared. I had heard that the best way to respond to a child's question about reproduction was to answer minimally but honestly, on the theory that the child will direct the conversation. "He's going to push his way out with his feet," I said.

My answer was accurate, if not confusing.

My daughter pressed me for more information, resulting in a lovely exchange about how he got inside me in the first place and what would happen when he arrived.

When I had explained as much as I thought my kindergartner needed to know, I reassured her that she had years of growing ahead of her before she would become a woman. "Your body will change in many ways, and as it does, you can always ask me about those changes and I can help you figure things out."

I thought I had given her plenty to mull over, but just in case, I left the door open. "Is there anything else you need to know right now?"

"Yes," she said, knitting her brows together in her most serious expression. She took my hand and gently traced my veins with her finger. "When does a woman get these veins that pop up on her hands? They're gross."

OK, so that was one question I hadn't anticipated.

I've learned much about how to present the "facts of life" since that first conversation with Katie. For one thing, I've learned that this is a conversation you must have over and over as children age. The lessons I taught my 5-year-old were just the beginning.

I've also learned that children don't ask as many questions as you think they will. If I waited for them to ask about sex, our conversations might be few and far between.

My second daughter was afflicted with an alarming lack of curiosity about human bodies and the origins of life. Worse, when Betsy was younger and I broached the subject, she covered her ears and sang loudly to block out the sound of my voice. I wasn't sure what she knew at that point, but apparently she thought it was enough.

By the time Betsy reached middle school, I had no choice but to force her to sit down to listen to some vital information – and quickly, before the sex education classes began on the school playground.

Once again, we're faced with initiating "the talk." The baby boy who prompted my eldest daughter's curiosity 11 years ago will enter the sixth grade in a few weeks, so I've been urging my husband to find the right moment for a frank discussion with him that will go into greater detail than the bits and pieces of information we've shared up to now. We think a man-to-man conversation is in order because I lack a good deal of direct experience with some of the issues they need to cover.

But instead of sitting our son down for some old-fashioned home-schooling on sex, my husband has consulted the dads of the other boys on his sports teams to determine whether they have yet to do the same.

It seems Jimmy and his friends are walking around in a fog of ignorance perpetuated by their fathers, who are convinced, to quote my husband: "The guys aren't ready."

Aren't ready for what? "We don't want to wait until they're married with children to tell them about sex," I said.

My husband, committed to giving our son a long and innocent childhood, thinks this information may send him too soon down the path to puberty.

On the other hand, I think when you're walking the prepubescent road, you ought to have some idea about the direction in which you're headed before your hormones start raging and you are suddenly, hopelessly lost.

Of course, there are plenty of people out there communicating with young people about sex, but the ones doing most of the talking are pop and rap singers, advertising executives, TV writers and Hollywood producers. Unfortunately, most of the time, these folks aren't sending messages I want my children to hear.

Not to mention, I suspect the images about sex portrayed through the media are a big reason children ask fewer questions than we expect they will. Children may be under the misguided notion they already are well-informed.

When it comes to teaching our children about sex, my husband and I walk the tightrope between innocence and ignorance. We respect their right and need to know about how their bodies will grow and develop. We want to reassure them that sexuality is natural and normal and good. We also want them to feel secure about where they came from.

But context is everything. In our home, when we talk about sexuality, we stress the moral and religious beliefs that inform our opinions about right behavior. We never offer information without strong messages regarding modesty, chastity, responsibility and respect.

Jim promises it's just a matter of finding the right moment this summer for "the talk" with Jimmy. Knowing my husband, that conversation will be filled with love and learning as he teaches our son not only the way boys grow, but what it really means to be a man.

Marybeth Hicks

When the caboose drives the train

Once again, I'm running late. It's 3:07, and by the time I turn into the school parking lot, the pick up line is a mile long and moving like molasses in winter. This is because all the "good" parents – the prompt ones – arrived at 2:45 in order to wait next to the curb.

Those of us who pull in just after the dismissal bell may as well wait until 3:20 to get here, since it'll take that long to reach the sidewalk.

I consider parking the van and walking across the lot to pick up my daughter, but the chances are good I'd be caught in a lengthy conversation with one of those "exceptional" parents who meet their children at the door.

This is too risky. These conversations usually mean I'll be forced to volunteer for something. I'm a reformed volunteer, so I don't get out of the car.

Instead, I inch forward, observing the various family dynamics as children disburse in clumps of two and sometimes three to rejoin their moms and dads for the ride home.

At last, I reach the curb. Only my second-grader waits for me – her older siblings stay after school for band and basketball practice. The automatic door on the van slides open and Amy bounds inside with an enthusiastic, "Hey, Mom."

"Guess what," she says. "Today in music class we got to sing songs that we made up, and I said I wanted to dedicate a song to all the kids who have older brothers and sisters. Want to hear it?"

"Of course," I say.

She clears her throat and finds her spot on the scale.

"I wish I was older than my brother, oh, yeah
I wish I was older than my brother, oh, yeah
I wish I was older than my brother, oh, yeah
I wish I was 22 and he was one."

She finishes with a long, soulful, warbling note. I resist the urge to laugh out loud. The song is funny, after all, but I don't want to encourage her too much. She's precocious enough as it is.

So I say, "Wow. What did your music teacher say?" I'm pretty sure this wasn't what he had in mind when he suggested the children sing for one another.

"He didn't really say anything," she replies. "But he did roll his eyes."

Why am I not surprised?

"What did the kids say?" I ask. I'm thinking maybe her performance fell flat, and she didn't notice

"Oh, they loved it," she says firmly, "especially the ones with big brothers."

"I wish I was older than my brother," is my daughter's anthem. Living as she does in the shadow of three older siblings, her existence feels like a series of rides in the van to events and activities in which she is not involved or included. She's the constant spectator at soccer games, basketball tournaments and cross-country meets, tagging along behind me, or more likely, trying breathlessly to catch up.

The reality is, this fourth child of mine is a little girl living in a world of teenagers and preteens. She says "cool, dude" when she likes something and when she feels oppressed by the big kids, she accuses them of "seeking world domination."

She knows the names of pop musicians and movies starring Lindsay Lohan. She watches old Mary-Kate-and-Ashley videos, but she knows they're really 18 now and one of them had an eating disorder.

When she plays dress up, her makeup job is a little too professional. She says when she grows up she wants to be a veterinarian or have her own cooking show on the Food Network.

In her heart, she wants to fit in among the giants around her. We're all amused at the dinner table when her unexpected quips hit the mark ("Kind of a lot of carbs tonight, huh, Mom?"), but we know it's not OK for her to behave like a miniature adult.

We want her to be sweet instead of savvy, but her reality includes experiences the others never encountered or imagined at her age. Can she help it if her older sister plays the flute in the marching band and she's forced to go to the high school football game on a Friday night?

Yet, an innocent childhood is her right and our responsibility.

Ironically, while she laments she's too young and unimportant, she has no idea of the vital role she plays precisely because she's our caboose.

When it feels like we're on the fast track to SATs and college tours, our little girl offers Saturday morning cartoons, reading aloud and sidewalk chalk.

When her siblings long for a break from responsibility, she's there for a round of pretend or a game of Guess Who?

When every square on the calendar forces us to eat on the fly and move through an endless series of commitments and scheduling conflicts, she's the reminder to go outside to play.

Except on Tuesdays. That's the day she has her own commitment – beginning jazz and tap – an hour each week her siblings can't claim.

There, in her black leotard, her tap shoes shining under the studio lights, my little one revels in the company of children just her size and takes her first steps toward a life of her own.

Marybeth Hicks

The weather (and the girls) are about to change

'Y ou guys ready for ice cream?" I ask my son and his buddy Eric as they approach the table. I'm sitting under an umbrella reading a book and chugging water while the boys try to stay cool in the pool, which feels more like a bathtub. It's about 95 degrees, and the trees are standing still.

The stifling air has had the boys swimming and splashing since we arrived at the swim club a couple of hours ago. As if on cue, they materialize every so often looking for handouts. First it was a lunch of chicken strips and fries; now it's time for the second course.

"Sure," Jimmy says. He flashes me a smile – the one he gives me when I suggest the very thing he hopes for before he even asks.

I watch Eric and Jimmy walk toward the snack shop, their wet feet leaving a path of footprints on the cement like imprints on a beach. They are both tall and lanky for their ages, but Eric is 18 months older and a year ahead in school. Their banter is drowned out by the shrieks of hundreds of children and the pool's mushroom fountain, an open-air shower that sounds like a broken water main.

The boys return with their frozen treats, eating greedily but with just enough reserve to avoid brain freeze. Having ordered a cone, not a cup, Eric finishes first and heads back to the pool.

"You guys having fun?" I ask my son as he finishes his ice cream.

"Yeah," he replies. An economy of words is the hallmark of a man.

"Eric's kind of a chick magnet," I observe. I've been watching the boys in the pool and have noticed a couple of middle school girls hanging around, making themselves obvious with some showy diving and the occasional overstated adjustment of a bikini top.

"Huh?" Jimmy asks. He hasn't noticed.

This is the difference between Jimmy – bound for sixth grade come the fall – and his buddy Eric, the soon-to-be seventh-grader. It's the difference between darkness and dawn, consciousness and a coma.

The difference is girls, the complicated people who one day will be the object of my son's unspoken preoccupation. For now, at the tender age of 11, the subject of girls has all the appeal of influenza.

"There are some girls in the pool who seem to be trying to get Eric's attention," I say. He looks at me with a face that is both clueless and uninterested.

I only broach this subject out of curiosity. I want to know where Jimmy lands on the Richter scale of interest in the fairer sex.

Clearly, Eric is aware there are girls in the pool who are sending signals in his direction. To his credit, he's pretending not to notice, possibly because it's apparent his buddy is oblivious. He's playing it cool. If he were spending the day with an older friend – say, someone approaching 13 – he might be engaged otherwise.

Already, the boy-girl thing has started a hormonal bolt of lightning through the telephone lines of several of my son's peers, according his classmates' parents. The girls think nothing of calling boys on a phony pretense such as asking about homeroom assignments for the coming year (never mind that classroom rosters for next year won't come out until late August – a fact they already know).

So far, the only time a girl called my son was when he hosted another boy for a sleepover. It turned out she was on the hunt for her real crush – our houseguest. I recall asking Jimmy what the call was about, and he answered, "I don't know." He really didn't know.

His ignorance won't last. There's about to be a seismic shift in my Jimmy's perceptions of the opposite sex. Up to now, the girls in my son's universe have served as a friendly oasis from the rough and rowdy pack with whom he generally plays. Girls tend to like school, and Jimmy likes school, too. Girls are clever and kind and often quiet. Girls laugh at his jokes; girls are nice.

Sadly, girls are about to change, the realization of which I suspect will overtake him like an earthquake, pulling the platform out from under the inexperienced, innocent footing on which he rests his understanding. Girls grow up faster than boys – that's just the way it is.

Already there are rumors of mixed groups of friends going to the movies together and of hand-holding. My young son is unlikely to be included in the groups that push the envelope of social development and less likely to go along if ever he were asked, assuming I would even permit such an outing (which I wouldn't).

I realize the day will come when his eyes will open to the allure of some preteen princess. It's inevitable. He'll glance her way, and she'll glance back. They'll exchange tentative smiles. He'll do something ridiculous to get her attention like attempt a handstand or snarf water out his nose or belch out a verse of *America the Beautiful* – something daring to demonstrate his machismo – and she'll think he is wonderful.

But not as wonderful as I think he is right now, unaware of the gale-force winds that will turn his head toward girls and away from the only woman who knows him through and through.

Whoever she is, she had better be something special because I'm not giving him up without a fight.

Marybeth Hicks

Growing confidence is always in style

I turned my back for only a moment, but that was all it took. As quickly as you can say "Vidal Sassoon," Michelle, the stylist cutting my daughter's hair, grabbed fistfuls of lovely brown locks and sliced vertically, a technique known in the hair business as "layering."

Never mind that it had taken months to grow my daughter's hair to one length – or that the haircut I had ordered was a "blunt bob."

Without thinking, I react. "What are you doing?" I gasp.

"You want it to curl under, don't you?" the stylist says defensively.

"I wanted it all one length – like the picture," I say, pointing to the larger-than-life poster of a model whose haircut we discussed mere minutes ago.

Michelle stops cutting, leaving roughly one third of Amy's head "blunt" and the rest freshly layered. Nervously, she fusses with Amy's hair, lifting it straight up and then tussling it as though playing with a puppy.

"Well, obviously, you have to cut the rest of it," I say. Michelle's hands shake as she works her way around my daughter's head, cutting varying lengths into her hair.

I watch in stunned silence for a few seconds, wondering where I'll find the time to blow-dry my 7-year-old's new high-maintenance haircut. Then I remind myself that it's only hair – it will grow.

"Don't you think I look cute, Mom?" Amy asks from under the enormous plastic tent hanging from her neck.

My eyes meet hers in the mirror. "You would look cute with purple spikes coming out of your head," I tell her, "and your haircut is adorable. I'm just worried we'll need extra time to fix it in the mornings before school." I'm also worried that it will look like wet spaghetti, but I don't say this.

"It's really short, but I like it," she says.

I realize that my reaction to the stylist is leading Amy to think her hair looks bad, so I pile on the compliments. "You know, now that I look at it, I can see it's going to be the cutest haircut ever," I say.

My positive spin works only until we get to the car. With the chilly air blowing on her newly exposed neck, she feels like a shorn sheep. "It's too short," she says as tears gather in her eyes. "I need you to get me a wig to wear to school tomorrow."

Hair is an issue about which I project my own humiliating past onto my present parenting. On at least three occasions, I endured haircuts that can only be described as "character building." One was a version of the '70s "shag" that looked enough like a mullet to require three remedial attempts to fix what was wrong. It might not have been so bad had this series of styles not inched their way up my scalp only a month before my sister's wedding, at which I looked like I wore steel wool atop my head.

So when my daughter pleads with me to stay home from school until her hair grows back, or at least for special permission to wear a hat during the school day, I empathize. "I know it feels different, but you'll get used to it. And the great thing is you're growing all the time – even your hair. Can't you feel it?"

"Everyone else has long hair," Amy wails. "I'm the only one with short hair. I look like a boy."

She doesn't even come close to looking like a boy, though saying so conjures memories of the hideous haircut I got in seventh grade. That was the time a girlfriend and I walked to Betty's House of Beauty and paid for radically short cuts with our baby-sitting money, leaving some 13 inches of femininity on the floor of the salon.

"Don't be silly," I say, uttering the most useless words in parenting. Crises in confidence aren't silly, but this is what parents say when we're out of ideas. "Your friends will love your hair, and besides, the only one who has to like it is you."

Visions of the "pixie" haircut I endured in third grade flood my consciousness. The style, inspired by '60s model Twiggy, is immortalized in my school photo. It's an image that suggests I had been playing with scissors.

A vague sense of discomfort causes me to indulge my daughter's hair anxiety a little longer. Then I say, "If you eat a lot of vegetables, it will grow more quickly." Why not use this event to my advantage, after all?

The next day, she checks her look in the rearview mirror before dragging her backpack out of the van. "Here goes," she says as she braces herself for what she's sure will be a difficult day.

Of course, her fears are unfounded. When I pick her up at 3, she skips to the van, her new hairstyle bouncing beautifully. "Everyone loved my hair," she says, beaming.

"See?" I say in my best I-told-you-so voice. "What did I tell you?"

"Actually, Mom, you told me not to worry because it will grow back," she says. "But I'm not worried because I like my hair."

What I said was that she is growing all the time – through an unexpected haircut or maybe because of one.

It turns out that with a blow dryer and a styling brush, Michelle was right. My daughter's hair curls under in the cutest bob, framing her face perfectly.

Then again, when she smiles, nobody notices her hair anyway.

Marybeth Hicks

Eavesdropping in the dark as son breaks speech barrier

Now for the rest of the story...

I am standing in the hallway outside my son's bedroom door, listening. OK, I'm eavesdropping – but it's the only way I'm going to find out what's really going on in his life.

Not that I don't ask him directly. Every afternoon in the van at the end of a long school day, I pitch questions such as, "What made today fun?" or "What happened that surprised you today?"

I've read parenting articles that recommend asking open-ended questions rather than those that can be answered with a simple "yes," "no" or the most meaningless reply, "fine." So, instead, I ask things that should elicit a thoughtful response.

Unfortunately, the answer I get from my son these days is "nothing."

How is this possible? He leaves the house before 8 a.m. and doesn't climb into the car until after 3 p.m. It's inconceivable to me that in more than seven hours away from home, nothing happens that is even remotely remarkable.

Yet, ever since he started sixth grade, I've noticed a change in Jimmy. The boy who can talk for seven or eight minutes without a breath about last week's soccer game or last night's Yankees game or the last frozen waffle in the refrigerator is suddenly mute about middle school.

When I ask, "Who did you hang with at recess?" the answer is, "My friends."

If I probe with, "Tell me about your classes," I get, "They're boring."

Once I asked, "So, do you have a girlfriend?"

He said, "No. Should I?" This felt like a conversational victory.

"Of course not," I said. "I just wanted to see what you'd say."

It seems unlikely that overnight my son has developed the male propensity for uncommunicativeness. His voice hasn't even started to crack, so it's too early for him to bury his face behind a newspaper and ignore the woman asking what he might like for dinner.

Besides, what I hear while standing in the dark is proof he's still talking. He's just not talking to me.

The whispered voices and muffled laughter are a sharp contrast to the busy, businesslike tone my son and I have adopted lately. Our time together is always short, often hectic – we interact in staccato, sharing cryptic messages to convey the bare essentials. It isn't talking so much as debriefing.

"Homework?" I ask.

"Science, lit and vocab," he says

"Got your gym clothes?"

"In my locker."

"Trombone?"

"Music room."

"Peanut butter?"

"Turkey. Cheese. No mayo."

It's not unfriendly, but it lacks depth, that's for sure.

This is why I'm so surprised when I hear the conversation between my husband and our son.

I'm in his room, hustling him along because he is well past his 9:30 bedtime. I grouse about the clothes on the floor, reminding Jimmy to bring his dirty laundry downstairs with him in the morning. I make a nagging comment about the pile of stuff on his desk and also about the unfinished book on his night table. I ask if he brushed his teeth and set his clock.

Then I tuck and kiss with maternal efficiency, already thinking about the chores that await me before I, too, can climb into bed.

Just before I leave the room, I pick a towel off the floor and head toward the bathroom to hang it on the towel rack. As I walk out, my husband comes in to say goodnight.

That's when I hear, "Sit down for a minute, Dad. I want to tell you about my day."

Unseen in the shadows, I freeze against the wall and listen to the animated, enthusiastic dialogue I have craved for nearly a month. Words tumble from my son's lips as he tells his dad everything I long to know about – the plot of the book he loves from literature class, a quiz he aced in math, a test to come in social studies – all the details that gave his day meaning and purpose. He did not do "nothing" but enjoyed a day filled with interesting ideas and challenging work.

When their conversation ends and their goodnights are said, I slip back into Jimmy's room and sit on the edge of his bed. I tell him I understand why he likes to talk to his dad, who is a great listener.

I tell him that our relationship is changing as he grows, as it should. It's natural for him to be closer to his dad as he gets older.

I remind him that he still can talk to me, too, even if most of our time together is rushed, our speech the familiar shorthand of daily conversation.

He gives me a hug, and we choke back a few tears. We both know it's inevitable that he will become the man he's meant to be, not the little boy who'll live forever in his mother's heart.

Then again, in the still of darkness, I discover there is much this boy will tell me when I stop and really listen.

Marybeth Hicks

When "going out" really means *going out*

'I have a question about boys," Amy says from the back seat of the van. "When I play with my Barbies and they go on dates to dinner or the movies, I say they're 'going out.' So why do kids say they're 'going out' with someone but they never go anywhere?"

The drive from school to our home covers just six miles, which doesn't give me much time to explain the adolescent mating process. "I think people say they're going out when they like someone and the person likes them back," I answer.

She sits quietly and absorbs this information. I imagine she's thinking about the Disney princesses and wondering why Sleeping Beauty never talks about how she's "going out" with Prince Charming.

Before I can change the topic from romance to homework, my eighth-grader pipes up with a story about a couple in her class who are going out – or are they breaking up? No one knows because it changes from hour to hour.

Talking with my daughters about boys gets more complicated all the time. Boys used to be just people – friends, even – we mentioned with the same casual interest with which we discussed movies, a math test or a hangnail.

All that has changed. Boys are either "yucky" (the second-grade conclusion) or "annoying" (the eighth-grader's assessment). Or else they're something we can't discuss, as in the case of my high school sophomore.

Somewhere between middle school and last week, my 15-year-old daughter decided 50 percent of the world's population is off-limits for conversation if the topic goes anywhere near her personal preference for one member of the male species over another.

Not that I sense she's all that interested in a serious romance. The young men in her universe walk on boat-size feet, bathe only sporadically and respond to conversation starters with monosyllabic grunts or a disgusted "whatever," leaving friendly girls such as my daughter to wonder why boys are so – what's the word I'm looking for? – unappealing.

This probably is the reason she's having a hard time deciding whom to invite to the upcoming Sadie Hawkins dance, the traditional "girl's bid" event at her high school.

You would think that in the post-feminist era, Sadie Hawkins would be a thing of the past. Certainly there's hardly a teenager in America who has any idea that Sadie

Hawkins was a creation of *Li'l Abner* cartoonist Al Capp.

Sadie was the "homeliest gal in the hills," the character in the *Li'l Abner* strip who got tired of waiting around for a suitor to "come a-courtin'." Sadie's pappy, Hekzebiah Hawkins, was even more worried about Sadie's prospects for marriage, so he declared "Sadie Hawkins Day" and devised a foot race in which the unmarried women of the town of Dogpatch chased down the local bachelors. If they caught 'em, they married 'em.

Back in 1937, when Al Capp unveiled Sadie's strategy for securing a husband, he inadvertently created an American folk event. In just a few years, schools all over the country had Sadie Hawkins Days that allowed the gals to choose their dates for dances and parties. According to the official *Li'l Abner* Web site, "It became a woman empowering rite at high schools and college campuses, long before the modern feminist movement gained prominence."

Sadie Hawkins Day was held annually in Mr. Capp's comic strip for 40 years and, incredibly, is still an event on some high school social calendars.

But whom to invite? I made the mistake of asking Katie this question a few nights ago. The dance is coming up soon, so it seemed like appropriate timing for her to arrange a date with a boy of her choosing.

The conversation didn't go as I expected. First, you would think I had asked the girl to reveal top-secret information that might compromise national security. Her face turned red, her eyes bulged from their sockets, and she puckered her lips as if she were sucking a lemon

"Mom," she wailed, "why are you asking me this question?

How should I answer?

Because I want to be sure the boy is someone we know and feel comfortable with?

Because I'm wondering if I can expect to spend an evening carting high school sophomores from dinner to a dance and home again?

Because I want to see her suffer the degradation and humiliation of discussing her social life with her mother?

I employed a time-tested parenting trick – I answered a question with a question: "Why are you making such a fuss?"

"Because you're embarrassing me," she whined.

I'm clueless. We were alone in the kitchen, so it wasn't as if someone was listening. Our conversation was no more embarrassing to me than if I had asked which flavor ice cream she wanted for dessert.

Obviously, I mistook my daughter for a regular person with whom I would have a normal conversation. I forgot that I was dealing with a 15-year-old girl and that we were talking about boys.

We had a mother-daughter chat about her plans for the dance. I tried to remember we're not girlfriends, which I work hard not to be, but I wish we could gush and giggle over the possible dates among the sophomore boys.

Of course, because I'm her mother, I think whomever she chooses for the Sadie Hawkins Dance will be pretty lucky.

That's probably what old Hekzebiah Hawkins thought, too.

Marybeth Hicks

Wisdom gained by accident makes for a safer driver

When the phone rang at 7:35 on a brilliant spring day, I knew it had to be one of two things. Either the mom down the block needed me to pick up her son for school, or something was wrong.

I was right. Something was wrong.

Katie and Betsy had left just five minutes earlier, 30 minutes ahead of the first hour bell, on a dry and sunny morning. With safe conditions and plenty of time to make the 10-minute drive to school, their risks were minimal. They were headed west, so even the sunshine wasn't a factor.

But somehow, they had an accident. Not a big one – no one was injured, thank the Lord. The only casualty was the little Honda Accord we had purchased five months earlier. On the advice of many experienced parents, we bought a car that could be considered "disposable."

When Betsy called, her voice told me all I needed to know. She was obviously upset, but there was no terror; no panic to convey a serious injury. She told me where they were and then hung up to call the police.

When I reached the four-lane highway near our neighborhood, a line of cars about a quarter-mile long clogged the road. Virtually all of those drivers shot me dirty looks (and a few expressive digits) as I peeled past them in the left shoulder.

There's no convenient way to say, "I'm the mother of the teenage driver who caused this backup." I forged ahead.

When the police officer arrived, Katie was ready with her tearful explanation. "I think something happened with the brakes," she said. "I slammed on them but ..." She trailed off in a look of disbelief and bewilderment.

The officer and I looked at Katie and then to the road leading up to her steaming, crumbled front fender. No skid marks.

Clearly, she was quite correct. There was a problem with her brakes – she didn't use them in time to avoid an accident.

(Just to be sure we hadn't permitted our daughter to take to the road in an unsafe vehicle, we asked a mechanic to confirm that the brakes worked before our former Honda made its weary way to the salvage yard.)

It took a day or two for the shock of losing the car to sink in. It also took about that long for me to get a true picture of what happened on the way to school that morning.

Getting accurate information from teenagers is easy if you watch enough *Law and Order* episodes. You learn a technique for drawing out the facts – keep asking the same question over and over, varying your phrasing just a bit. Gradually, you uncover details that explain everything.

This is how I found out about the Chap Stick.

Katie had used Chap Stick while sitting at a red light. She dropped the top between the two bucket seats and enlisted her sister to find it. Apparently Betsy didn't take as much interest in finding the top as Katie would have preferred.

By the time they reached the next light, Katie's focus was off the road just long enough to miss the cue conveyed by the brake lights in front of her.

Then, BAM. One minute she's driving, the next we're waving goodbye as the tow truck drags the car to "vehicular afterlife."

It's not as if we didn't discuss the potential for being distracted prior to her becoming a licensed driver. We told Katie how easy it is to divert your focus when you're behind the wheel and we made rules to help minimize distractions, such as no passengers other than her sister and no using the cell phone while she drove.

We forgot to mention Chap Stick.

Of course, we didn't mention a host of things that might take her mind off the road, from biology tests and French assignments to birds in the air and cute guys walking along the roadway. We trusted that she appreciated how critical it is to pay close attention when you're operating a machine as potentially dangerous as an automobile.

This week we finally replaced the third car in our driveway. We had decided not to rush into purchasing another auto – for one thing, there was the money. We also waited until we felt sure Katie had absorbed all the wisdom her driving mishap offered.

She certainly isn't alone in learning the pitfalls of inattention with first-hand experience. According to the National Safety Council, a driver's crash risk is at a lifetime high in the first 12 to 24 months of driving, and one estimate puts the number of new drivers involved in reportable traffic accidents at 14 percent.

Thankfully, the accident my daughter reported was just a fender-bender, and better, the only fender bent beyond repair was ours. In the end, Katie's inattention cost her merely the convenience of having a car at her disposal for a few months.

For some teens, the price of distraction is much higher. The NSC says traffic accidents remain the leading cause of death for Americans aged 15 to 20. While teens account for only 7 percent of drivers, they comprise roughly 14 percent of traffic fatalities.

Knowing these statistics – and many of the stories of grief behind them – makes me unspeakably grateful we have a reason to replace that first car at all.

Marybeth Hicks

The playground is paved with good intentions

They'll be giving you the "Think Sheet" for this, Gandhi.....

immy's chin quivers, his lower lip and thin voice trembling as he speaks. "This was the second-worst day of fifth grade," he says, climbing into the van. His eyes pool with tears, but he's trying hard to choke them back.

"Wow. That's bad," I sympathize. The first-worst day happened just a week ago, when his basketball team lost a one-point game and was eliminated from the post-season tournament. That was a bad day. I can only imagine what this one entailed.

"I had to go to Mr. J.'s office," he confesses. My son begins a lengthy – if somewhat disjointed – explanation of a playground scuffle that includes a stolen basketball, repeated pleas for its return and the use of the word "sissy."

I listen intently as I pull out of the after-school pickup line and turn into the parking lot. "Let's go inside to see Mr. J., and you can both tell me what happened."

Clearly, if I'm going to get any accurate information, I'll need an adult perspective. Not to mention, my son's not exactly objective. He wouldn't last 30 seconds in Bill O'Reilly's *No Spin Zone*.

"Mr. J." – "The J. Man," "The J. Dawg," students have many names for him – is the assistant principal. His job includes a wide range of roles, from disciplinarian to mediator to sounding board. Melees on the playground are one of his specialties.

When we knock on his door, Mr. J. waves us in, and we take seats around the small table in the center of his office. We all agree that getting in a fight at lunchtime is out of character for Jimmy, who, though not a pacifist, is wise enough to see there are unpleasant consequences to the rough-and-tumble life – such as pain.

Jimmy reiterates, rephrases, revises and repeats his version of the story, which essentially puts him in the role of misguided advocate for the "victim," his buddy Michael. Michael "had the ball first," "didn't do anything" and "was only standing there." This doesn't explain why Jimmy felt the need to hold back Michael and the other boy involved in the mishap to keep them from pounding the stuffing out of each other.

We discuss whether Jimmy had alternatives to diving into a fistfight. I suggest that because the adult supervisor on the playground saw the entire incident, perhaps my son could have called on him to help rather than assume the role of "recess vigilante."

Jimmy tries again to replay the skirmish, as though a more thorough explanation will help me understand why his response was reasonable. Mr. J. says things like, "It sounds like you wanted to defuse the situation. That's good. But what else could you have done besides get in the middle of a fight?"

Mr. J. explains that my son and the other boys must complete a "Think Sheet," a worksheet designed to reassess one's actions and devise a plan for the future that avoids playground combat. They also will serve as table washers in the cafeteria for a week, a natural consequence because it cuts their playtime short.

When we get up to leave his office, Mr. J. says, "Every mistake is a learning opportunity." He's a big fan of "the teachable moment," and thank goodness, because his days are filled with them.

Jimmy slumps his shoulders forward and hangs his head low as we walk back to the van. "Why are you so upset?" I ask him. It's clear the assistant principal believes he meant well, even though he made a bad decision. "Everybody makes mistakes."

He can't really articulate his feelings, but I get that Jimmy's sad because he believes he was unjustly accused. "I didn't do anything," he keeps saying, though clearly he did do something. The part where he admits shoving another boy shows there obviously is an infraction, and I'm the kind of mom who believes there's always more to the story than what I hear.

On the drive home, we talk about the difference between actions and intentions – a key concept when teaching accountability. "Nobody can judge your intentions," I explain. "You might have been thinking, 'Here's my chance to win a Nobel Peace Prize by breaking up this fight,' but the playground monitor can't read your mind. He can only watch you jump in the middle of an argument and assume that's what you meant to do."

I tell him I believe he meant to break up the fight, but that ultimately, he's accountable for his actions. He stares out the window and heaves a resigned sigh.

I decide to cheer him up. "And anyway," I point out, "there's no way this was the second-worst day in fifth grade. It's not nearly as bad as the day you gave your speech in social studies and you were the only person without note cards or a visual aid." Somehow, he's not uplifted.

Later that night, he brings me the completed Think Sheet and a pen so I can sign it. He has described his actions, his intentions and his alternatives for the future in a way that tells me he understands what he did wrong.

I give him an encouraging smile and say, "Let's make this the last trip to Mr. J.'s office, OK?"

But I know better. There are too many teachable moments in his future to keep him from visiting "The J. Dawg."

Marybeth Hicks

Fame and fortune – maybe

Honey.... I'm home...!

You can learn a lot about children by asking what they'd like to be when they grow up.

Back in kindergarten, my son told us he wanted to be a priest. I thought this was wonderful – a reflection of his budding spirituality and faith in God. Turns out he was simply attracted to the idea that he wouldn't have to get married.

"I don't want a wife telling me what to do," he said – as if he had ever seen such a wife. Hmmm.

As he got older, his goal changed. One morning over breakfast, he said he no longer wanted to be a priest. "Really?" I asked "What made you change your mind?"

"I want to be the bishop. He doesn't have a wife telling him what to do, plus he's the one to tell all the other priests what to do. It's a better job."

That goal lasted about a week. Next thing we knew, Jimmy declared his plan be become the pope.

"Oh, I get it," my husband said. "He wants to go into politics." We all started calling him "Il Papa" for a while, until his dream evolved again.

Now he wants to play in the NBA. Of course, because he's just 10, anything is possible.

At dinner recently, I conducted an updated survey on the career plans of our four children.

This is a good way to get a handle on their sense of purpose, not to mention it's a reality check on our college savings plan. We figure anyone older than 11 who considers the medical profession as an option might be serious. That would make things more expensive for us than, say, having a child who longs to sell insurance.

Unfortunately, none of them ever talks about selling insurance. I don't know why not. Some of the happiest and most prosperous people I know are my insurance professionals. Plus, they play a lot of golf. This seems like a great career.

On the other hand, having a child in the medical profession would be convenient, to say the least. Who wouldn't want her son or daughter to be a doctor, especially at 10:30 at night when your sinuses are clogged and the idea of a trip to the urgent care center brings tears to your already watery eyes?

But medicine is out. When we told them how many years of school it would take to become a doctor, they all said, "No, thanks."

Unless you count my youngest daughter, who still talks about becoming a veterinarian. She might be well-suited to this job, as she's the only one who can stand the smell when we walk into our vet's office. Mostly, I think her dream of becoming a vet is a reflection of her love for Scotty, our dog.

In any case, being a vet is just a backup plan, on the outside chance she doesn't make it as a runway model. She recently started practicing her "strut" around the house.

The dinner-table conversation yielded this update: One ubermodel; one Detroit Pistons shooting guard; one nationally recognized, award-winning journalist; and a chef (a career inspired by Betsy's most treasured 13th birthday gift – her very own George Foreman grill).

It's not enough to know what they want to be when they grow up. I needed to know why. Is it notoriety they're after? Money? Power? Interestingly, all of their choices have the potential for fame and fortune, leading me to question whether we're instilling the proper values about work.

"Well," Amy explained, "when you pick a job, you should choose something you love and that you're really good at. I think I will be really good at modeling because I am beautiful and also, I can do this." Whereupon she jumped out of her chair for a demonstration, pulling her shoulders back, sucking in her cheeks and catwalking around the kitchen.

She wasn't bad, actually. We all praised the way she made her "Big Dog" T-shirt look like the latest fashion from Milan.

One by one, our children offered justifications for their future career paths, but the basic premises were pretty much the same – a combination of aptitude and desire.

"What if you love something but you're not that good at it?" I asked.

"If you love something, like art or cooking or sports, you can get good at it if you do it a lot," Katie said. "The important thing is to do something that makes you happy because that's going to be the thing that's most likely to be successful."

And what about fame and fortune? The short answer – yes. They all dream of reaching the pinnacle of their professions, and they all want big bucks. For what it's worth, they promise my husband and me glamorous vacations and sports cars and to pay off our present mortgage.

We'll be happy if they just make enough money so they don't have to come back as adults and live in our basement.

What did my informal survey around the dinner table reveal? Unfettered optimism. Uninhibited self-confidence. Unbridled imagination. As I sat listening to their plans, it occurred to me those are just the things our world needs most.

I admit their present passions won't necessarily change the world, but I'm not concerned. Tomorrow, they'll probably dream of something different.

Marybeth Hicks

Weekend together is a window to our future

No hurry...

"**G**umball machines or pinball machines?" Amy breaks the easy silence of our twilight car ride by continuing the game we've been playing all weekend.

"Gumball machines," I say. "My turn. A hike in the woods or a walk on the beach?"

She answers with no hesitation. "A walk on the beach."

I knew she would say that.

It had been a long, lazy weekend of questions and answers as my youngest daughter and I enjoyed a "Mom and Amy adventure."

The opportunity to go away together wasn't planned; it appeared on our summer calendar by serendipity. I had signed up to help transport our older daughters' high school cross country team to camp – a four hour drive north. Only I didn't drive any team members, just their luggage. This left an empty seat for Amy, and an excuse to take my eight-year-old on an overnight excursion, (leaving my husband at home with our son).

I figured the time alone together would give me the chance to bond with my baby; to learn even more about my youngest child, so often the tag-along on the grown-up activities of her busy siblings.

We didn't map out our trip. Instead, after delivering a vanload of suitcases and sleeping bags to their rightful owners, we put our fingers to the proverbial wind. "Let's start looking for a hotel," I suggest.

The first thing I learn is that Amy prefers luxury accommodations.

"How about that one?" She points up the driveway of an exclusive resort.

"We're looking for something a bit more affordable," I say. Note to self: Must work with this child on setting realistic expectations.

Before long – and only after I reassure Amy of its safety and cleanliness – we check into a modest hotel.

The weekend unfolds in unhurried and effortless fun. Miniature golf (she had two holes in one, but I prevailed overall); staying up late to watch the Food Network's *Iron Chef America*, church on Sunday morning, brunch at an outdoor café.

Eventually the day finds us on a lake beach, where Amy bounces from the playground to the water's edge while I watch her and wonder how my motherhood job could have changed so quickly and so profoundly.

Suddenly, I realize I am spending the weekend in my future.

After years of traveling in a perpetual pack with my four children, traipsing en mass from the grocery store to the park to the pool, conquering errands in the midst of a boisterous bunch that often seems larger than the just four people to whom I gave birth, I'm down to only one child.

"Do you realize," I say to her at the end of our beach day, "this is the first time in 14 years I've spent a day alone on a beach with one of my children? The last time was with your big sister Katie – who was only two years old at the time."

"Wow. I'm pretty lucky," she says.

"Indeed," I say. Yet most of the time, I don't think so.

Most of the time I feel guilty for schlepping this child to every basketball game, track meet, play practice and teacher conference on our family calendar – very few of which involve her. In truth, she spends a lot of time complaining about her life as the caboose on our collective train, and I can't blame her.

Being the youngest in a large family means waiting to be one of the "big kids," though this never actually comes to pass, since no matter how old you get, the family members ahead of you already are blazing new trails. It's an exercise in frustration, to say the least.

But now, borrowing a page from the future we are yet to enjoy together, I finally get that her life as the youngest isn't so bad after all.

On the one hand, she's experiencing a loud and loving home where two sisters and a brother "torment" her with teasing and tickles.

On the other hand, those older siblings will fly the coop before we know it, leaving this last chick the undivided attention of a mom and dad who aren't in any hurry to inhabit an empty nest.

When you look at it this way, she has the best of both worlds.

To be sure, it's lonelier for Amy than it was for her siblings when they were her age. Rather than play on the beach with a built-in band of buddies, she circled the swing set looking for a welcoming smile. But in this she's gaining the confidence to strike out and make new friends – something that doesn't come as naturally to her older sibs.

My pondering about the changing nature of my family fades with the orange summer sky. We're making the trip back home, drifting in and out of conversation. For a while it's quiet and I figure she's asleep, since the only sound is the hum of the tires on the highway.

Then, from the back of the van, Amy says, "Chocolate or vanilla?"

We agree on chocolate, of course.

Marybeth Hicks

No avoiding the saddest day of summer

Moving day has been a long time coming. Our neighbor was transferred at the end of last summer because of an unexpected promotion. With four children – including a high school senior – it didn't make sense to pick up stakes and relocate the entire family just a few weeks before the school year began, so his wife and children stayed behind.

Their decision to postpone their move and endure a family separation for the sake of a job created a challenging circumstance for our friends, but it meant the complexion of our neighborhood wouldn't change right away.

Football games still would be played on their front lawn.

Halloween still would mean bounding in the darkness from house to house.

The first snow still would find my children and their pals from across the street sliding down the hill in our back yard.

Despite the plans that clearly were under way, it was possible to deny the day when our neighbors would move away and, more poignantly, the day Kaylan would leave the neighborhood.

Kaylan is Amy's anchor; the truest thing she knows about herself is that she is Kaylan's best friend, even when her best friend likes playing soccer with the boys down the street more than she likes playing dolls in Amy's pink bedroom.

They took ballet and jazz together. They rode the first-grade bus together. They walk their dogs together. They sometimes have been inseparable; they always have been devoted. They share a loyalty that comes when you meet in preschool and grow into girlhood together.

Unfortunately, the seasons changed quickly and reliably. By the time the crickets buzz and the sound of firecrackers signals the Fourth of July weekend, moving day will have come and gone.

A team of burly guys in matching shirts will make countless trips across our neighbor's front lawn, packing a trailer with furniture and boxes and bicycles. When they finish loading, they'll drive away, our friends following them up the street in their family car, leaving my 8-year-old daughter with a heart as empty as the house they called home.

When we first learned the move was imminent, Amy took it hard. I managed to persuade her to stay focused on the present – the months when her first, best friend would remain just a barefoot sprint across the street.

"It's a whole school year," I said. "You'll spend your birthdays together and have sleepovers and play outside. Nothing is changing yet, so don't be sad before you have to."

That strategy worked until our neighbors listed their house for sale in January and the sign went up on their front lawn, serving as Amy's daily reminder that the end eventually would come.

(Oddly, the banner on the sign with the Realtor's name and phone number never seems to be in place, causing me to wonder if my daughter is a saboteur. Maybe she thinks the move is predicated on selling the house.)

Now, with the leaves dancing in the warm breeze and the lazy rhythm of summer taking hold, Amy has started to face the sadness she has dreaded for so long. Kaylan really is leaving.

About a week ago, Amy curled up on the couch under her favorite blanket, claiming she didn't feel good. She doesn't feel good a lot these days, and I imagine her stomach anxiously churns the way we all feel when we confront something bad that is beyond our control.

I sat on the edge of the couch and pretended to take her temperature by kissing her forehead. "I don't think you're sick," I said. "I think you're sad."

We both knew what I meant. Suddenly, she started to cry with a depth of grief I'm not sure she knew she felt. Her little body heaved in my arms as she poured out the loss of the friend who taught her what it meant to be a friend.

I didn't tell Amy not to cry. I had been telling her to hold back her tears for so many months, and finally the time had come to put them on my shoulder where they belonged.

But I did tell her it would be OK. "I know this is going to be hard for you," I said, "We all know that. But we're all here for you, and I promise you it's going to be all right."

I might have expected her to argue my prediction – to tell me I was wrong; it wouldn't be OK. But instead, she put her wet face next to my ear and whispered through her tears, "Mom, how do you know?"

I couldn't begin to answer her; I didn't know how to articulate my certainty that her heart would heal, allowing her to find and keep a lifetime of friends within the many layers it grows as years unfold.

I just know.

"You'll have to trust me on that," I said.

I wish I could spare Amy the moment when our neighbors drive away and she must wave goodbye to her friend, remaining on the sidewalk to accept the lonely reality that awaits her, but such is life.

Friends move away, and we have to say goodbye.

It turns out that the hardest thing about being a parent isn't keeping your child's heart from breaking. The hardest thing is knowing your child's heart must break and waiting on the front porch while it happens.

Marybeth Hicks

Marybeth Hicks

Einstein's mother's
theory of relativity

Marybeth Hicks

Einstein's mother's theory of relativity

There are only 11 days until the science fair – the dreaded, unholy science fair – bane of English-major mothers from coast to coast.

Already, we're way behind.

The chatter in the school parking lot about exhibits started weeks ago. Some families anticipate the science fair all year, contemplating various topics to investigate and ways to report the results of experiments. They wonder for months what would happen if they place a balloon over the mouth of a 2-liter bottle of Diet Coke, or what color birdseed sparrows prefer, or whether an ice cube melts faster in air or water.

The science fair asks burning questions such as: Which cheese grows mold fastest? What happens to your gums when you floss them? Do bananas brown faster on the counter or in the refrigerator?

Not to mention, the science fair offers the opportunity to use the four steps of the scientific method: observation, hypothesis, prediction and testing.

Science fairs celebrate the process of discovery. Against the canvas of the physical world, science fairs invite children to capture the beauty of our surroundings. They offer the chance to turn a tri-paneled piece of corrugated cardboard into a virtual laboratory. With a little Elmer's glue, a magazine, a pair of scissors, some Styrofoam balls and a length of twine, a child unlocks a secret of the cosmos.

I wonder if the theory that children learn science by participating in a fair was ever tested with the scientific method? Someone should revisit this hypothesis, because based on my observation, the science fair is really just a tool to sift out the scientific, left-brained parents from the unscientific, right-brained types. Its real purpose is not educational, but rather psychological – to ferret out and expose those of us who don't actually know everyday science.

For example, many parents understand how electricity travels from their utility bill to the outlets on the walls of their homes. They explain energy to their children, who then create tabletop replicas of Niagara Falls, which they bring to the science fair and generate enough electricity to light the gymnasium for a month.

These are the parents whose children will never take home a measly "participant" ribbon. They're in it for "Best of Fair."

Now, I don't want to seem cynical, but I strongly suspect that some of our budding scientists are not, in fact, conducting their experiments entirely on their own. Of course, an appropriate amount of parental supervision is necessary and expected; but honestly, when a second-grader comes in with a miniature superconducting cyclotron made of Legos, you have to wonder, "Does little Sarah really know how to split atoms?"

Sure, a third-grader may be interested in thermodynamics; it's just that I have my doubts about how many can design a steam-powered rocket boat without help from mom or dad – on a school night, no less.

Every year, the science fair seems to get bigger and more elaborate. Long tables line the gym with numbered spaces, color coded for every grade. Even the kindergarten has a table. In kindergarten, all of life is a petri dish for the germ population found on sticky hands. Who needs an experiment? When you're 5, lunch is a science project.

Of course, one fifth-grade boy always brings the obligatory volcano, oozing with fake lava, demonstrating not only the geologic wonder of eruption but also the capacity of some parents to mold chicken wire and mix globs of papier-mache.

At my house, science projects are limited to whatever we can discover by using things found in our kitchen cupboards. Unfortunately, this means sometimes we study phenomena such as, "How many people prefer basil over oregano?" (For purposes of the science fair, six is a statistically significant sample).

Perhaps if I were remotely scientifically inclined, my children's science fair entries would be more gripping than comparing the weights of breakfast cereals (with and without milk), or which takes longer to chew, raisins or carrots.

Our projects never need time to gestate, incubate or ferment; they don't require hot pads or dry ice; they never involve fire. We don't need signs next to our posters warning, "Stand back" or "Don't try this at home." You can't get hurt looking at a jar of popcorn that reveals how many kernels didn't open in the microwave, after all.

I realize I may be stifling my children from developing their inner Einsteins, but I don't think Einstein's mother was very happy about the mess in her kitchen either. And based on my observations about science fairs, she may well have been the actual author of the theory of relativity.

Then again, nobody will ever wonder if my children did their own experiments – proving that while I may be unscientific, at least I know the science fair is not intended to display my aptitude for chemistry or physics or biology. It's not even intended to display my children's aptitude.

Rather, the science fair stands as an annual proclamation that children should enjoy a sense of wonder about the world around us. It's a chance to nurture their natural curiosity – to explore the simple principles that combine to form the most complex, miraculous creation ever devised – our universe.

The science fair asks "Why?" and offers answers beyond my uninformed, "Because that's how God made things."

Hey, I know it's not scientific, but most of the time, it's the best I can come up with.

Marybeth Hicks

Who knew you'd need Algebra later in life?

The afternoon routine hums along like clockwork. At the sound of the 3 p.m. bell, three of my four kids joined their sports teams for practice. Two hours later, sweaty and tired, they've peeled off their stinky socks and wadded them into aromatic balls on the floor next to their backpacks.

How they can concentrate with that odor hanging in the air, I'll never know, but they unload the night's assignments and crack the books.

The school year is only a month old and already the homework is breathtaking. Tonight, my daughter the sophomore has assignments in theology, U.S. history and geometry. Before bed, she'll read several chapters of *The Scarlet Letter*, due next week.

The eighth-grader just finished her social studies assignment – finding a map online depicting the Louisiana Purchase. She joins her sister in the living room where textbooks and notebooks cover the couch and litter the floor.

At the kitchen table, my fifth-grade son works on a page of English sentences due tomorrow. Even my second-grader has homework – looking up "key words" in the glossary of her literature book.

Everybody seems to have things under control. I'm supervising and answering questions while I start dinner.

And then, I hear the words every English major mother dreads: "I need help with my algebra."

Even in high school, I could sooner write an essay about algebra than do it. Algebra is one of those subjects I thought you didn't need to learn because you'd never use it again. Turns out you do need algebra – when your kids take it and ask you to help them with their homework.

In our household, math dispelled the myth that "Mom knows everything." Used to be I could dazzle my kids with answers to their every question. Why do avocados have pits? To grow new ones. Prepositions? I know 40 by heart. Photosynthesis? I can spell it and explain it.

But math is another story. I'm good through long division, but once we get to fractions, I say things like, "I've been to fifth grade. It's your turn to figure out the answers." (Mom-speak for "please don't make me sit down and try to remember how to find the common denominator.")

The Mom Mythology unraveled completely when Katie reached middle school and brought home her first "logic puzzle." If a man is stranded on an island with six sheep and a boat that seats only five, how many trips must he make with the fox until all the sheep are sweaters?

Where do they come up with this stuff? And what does it have to do with math? It's not logical anyway. Why not just shoot the fox or take a ferry? Plus, there's only one right answer and in my house, we're usually up until about 10:45 trying to find it.

So just now, when the call for help comes from the living room, I deflect (in an effort to teach the children the important leadership skill of delegation). "Help Betsy with her math," I say to Katie.

"It's not math, it's algebra." I stand corrected.

"Excuse me, algebra," I say.

They put their heads together over the book, but right away it's clear the younger sibling isn't interested in solving the problem. She's just looking for sympathy. She does what any eighth-grade girl will do in this situation – she gets huffy and emotional.

"This isn't the way my teacher did it," she whines

"Maybe not, but we weren't in your algebra class this morning, so you'll have to do the problem the way your sister is explaining it." I'm trying to stave off an argument between the two of them and hold back some mathematically induced tears before dinner

"I have to do it the way she taught us," she wails.

"Then you'll have to call someone who's in the class with you or else use the process your sister is explaining. But fussing and whining aren't going to get the homework done." Who says I can't do logic?

I look at the clock and realize if she doesn't conquer the algebra soon, my husband will step in the door and we're in for a tense 20 minutes. It's not that he minds helping with homework – in fact, he enjoys it. It's a great way for him to keep tabs on what the kids are learning. But dads, teenaged girls and math are a combustible combination sure to end in tears and frustration – for her, too.

She stews for a few minutes. Then, with an age-appropriate mood swing, she brightens and announces, "I did it."

Turns out she remembered how the teacher solved the problem on the board this morning. Or else she actually looked in the book without my noticing. Either way, the algebra is done and she's moving on to literature.

"I knew you could figure it out," I say confidently.

It's times like these, when I can't offer any help, I wish math had come more naturally to me, just to perpetuate the myth I always know what I'm talking about.

Then again, if I'd been able to help my daughter tonight, she'd have relied on me and not on her own ability to think through the problem. Instead, she proved to herself that when she sticks with it, she can find the answer.

Not to mention, she got it right.

Marybeth Hicks

Mom's right again. Go figure.

Aren't you tired of always being right....?

No... just tired.

When you're a parent, it's no consolation that you're right most of the time.

Case in point: When Katie told me on Friday that she had two papers to write for her British literature class, one due Monday and the other due Tuesday, I said: "That's physically impossible."

She already was committed to be in the school drama production both Friday and Saturday nights and to play her flute in the band festival on Saturday morning. Subtract an hour for church and four hours for the cast party on Sunday (impossible to skip because we were hosting it at our house), and what she had were approximately 10 scattered hours in which to write two major essays.

Anyone could see I was right – anyone, that is, except a teenager with a habit of underestimating the time it takes to do things.

"It's not a problem," Katie protested. "I already have all my quotes picked out from *Hamlet,* and I know what my thesis is for the second paper."

Spoken like a girl who will be surprised to find herself sitting at a computer after midnight in a quiet, dark house, watching Sunday melt into Monday as she types furiously under the glow of a weary desk lamp.

Of course, this isn't the first time she has put off completing a major project until the last minute, nor is it the first time I've cautioned her about the perils of procrastination. For reasons I can't fathom, my incessant nagging of my teenage daughter about time management hasn't worked. Go figure.

If logic prevailed, my 16-year-old scholar would listen thoughtfully when I offer insights on how to parcel out the precious little time available to her so she can meet her deadlines and still eat, sleep and bathe (bathing losing its importance as the weekend ekes away).

Absurd, I know. Not to mention, I can hear my mother six states away laughing as she reads this. Apparently, as a teenager, I was similarly afflicted with an unwavering belief in my dominance over the clock.

I suppose if I knew then what I know now, I would have been a 45-year-old high school junior. Wisdom and experience don't come any way other than simply from living one year to the next.

Still, it's the responsibility of all parents to impart our wisdom to our children, even as we expect them to test our advice to see if we're really right about things. After all, everyone makes mistakes – even parents. Children must figure the odds are good that mom and dad are just overprotective, risk-averse fun repellents.

Not so, of course – but again, being right is little comfort.

For example, I was right about the cost of replacement retainers – $390. I also was right when I said leaving your retainers on a paper napkin next to your lunch bag (as opposed to putting them in the case in your locker) would put said retainers at risk for the trash can.

I was right when I said doing tricks on a scooter was dangerous and ill-advised. My son gained this wisdom on his own, however, when he attempted a scooter jump and took out the better part of his two front teeth.

(I am right when I remind my children that anytime you hear someone say "Watch this trick," pain follows.)

I was right when I said putting the miniature MP3 player in the pocket of your jeans would result in a broken – albeit clean – MP3 player. I was right again when I said it about the replacement player.

I am always right about the relationship between leaving the kitchen to watch TV while you are cooking and burning food on the stove.

The impact of spilled Diet Cherry Coke on a laptop keyboard? I was right about that. (I also was right about the response my daughter could expect from her dad when he found out his laptop was ruined.)

The impact of your bumper on the car ahead of you when you don't leave adequate following distance? Boy, was I right about that.

It's not that I'm self-satisfied about being right so much of the time. In fact, I would much rather be wrong. It would be cheaper, anyway.

Suffice to say, I wish I were wrong about the time it takes to write papers for school. Looking at the circles under the tired eyes of my high school junior, I would give anything to have been the one who guessed incorrectly about the time it takes to do things.

We all have to endure our share of missed deadlines, capped teeth and burned bacon to create our personal books of wisdom. As much as I would love to spare my children the grief and frustration their decisions might cause them – as often as I'm right – there are no life lessons as compelling as the ones they'll teach themselves.

That's a pearl of wisdom about which I'm absolutely, positively right.

Marybeth Hicks

Perfect advice from one imperfect mom to another

The e-mail from my girlfriend didn't come with an electronic red flag or even the letters "SOS" in the subject line, but it was filled with urgency nonetheless.

"Give me some words of wisdom, because I actually am overwhelmed to the point of panic about all the excess details school adds to our day," Kathleen wrote. Her older daughter recently started kindergarten, and Kathleen is fast discovering this is nothing like preschool.

I guess she figures I've made it this far – two children in high school, one in middle school and one in third grade, so I'm wise, if not battle-weary.

It turns out my friend's panic isn't really over the new scheduling demands but the emotional demands of keeping up with other moms. "Will we be school pariahs if we don't attend the ice-cream social next week? Will the 'perfect' moms know I'm buddying up to them just because I may need their help someday? Will they hold it against me if I do?"

Kathleen is a single adoptive mom of two little girls who takes care of her daughters while also working full time as a news reporter. She manages to hold it all together with Band-Aids, love and a great sense of humor. However, she has discovered what experienced moms like me have known for a long time: There are Perfect Mothers, and if you compare yourself to them, you'll feel inadequate at best. At worst, you'll think you're a failure.

Perfect Mothers are those well-dressed, neatly coifed, perpetually organized women who juggle motherhood, volunteering, socializing, shopping, family commitments and jobs, all of which they handle with military precision and sweet, lipsticked smiles. These women are remarkable, but they make some of us uneasy.

You may not notice them until you're part of a school community. Perfect Mothers are the ones who orchestrate and attend every class party, field trip and committee meeting. Perfect Mothers' names populate the lists of indispensable people who raise money and coordinate teacher gifts and work in the school library several times each week.

Perfect Mothers are cheerful. They are charming. They even are physically fit.

They are perfect.

Obviously, I must not seem like one of these women if Kathleen chose me as her mentor in imperfection – and of course, she's right.

I mull over her observations about Perfect Mothers while I sit at my cluttered desk, surrounded by the piles of paper representing the many layers in the onion that is my life.

One pile deals with my two younger children, another pile is for the older ones. There is a pile of notes about events I still must incorporate into our master schedule; a pile of receipts and bills I'm trying to ignore; a pile of work-related reading; a pile of letters awaiting replies.

I can't really see what's in any of the piles because my reading glasses are buried under one of them. Despite the obvious chaos in front of me crying out for attention, I can't resist dashing off an answer to my friend.

"You're right that kindergarten is different from preschool, especially where the moms are concerned," I write back. "There are a good number of women who take their roles as school volunteers/standard-bearers of perfection very seriously. I spend a lot of time feeling sheepish while repeating my mantra, 'I'm doing the best I can.'"

I give Kathleen permission to skip the ice-cream social. I tell her it's a good idea to cop a healthy attitude about these things early in her daughter's school career. "Only do what makes sense for you and your family," I say, as though I have followed this advice myself.

In reality, I repeatedly overextend myself in a vain effort to keep up with the women whose levels of participation far surpass my capacity for multitasking.

I know why Kathleen is stressed. Comparing ourselves to other women, we can't help but assume they're better at everything – even at mothering their children. They do everything with such competence – panache, even – not to mention, in shoes that match what they're wearing.

Many mornings I compare myself to Perfect Mothers as I whip through the drive-through drop-off before making a hasty exit from the school grounds. I don't want to be seen because I may or may not have taken a shower (though let me just state for the record I will always have brushed my teeth, just in case I get pulled over by the police). If I haven't showered, I will be sporting "bedhead." If I have, my hair may be wet and profoundly unattractive. Either way, I'm far from perfect.

Kathleen sends another e-mail to update me on her assimilation into the school community.

"It's like attending an uncomfortable cocktail party without the benefit of a cocktail. I decided I would make it my policy to approach the people who looked as uncomfortable as I felt. That worked pretty well, proof yet again that coping is what moms do," she wrote.

Indeed. Coping is what all moms do, and the truth is, nobody's perfect.

Our e-mail exchange reminds me of a plaque I once saw in the kitchen of a wise friend. It says: "Comparison is the killer of contentment." Compared to the Perfect Mothers, moms like Kathleen and me may always come up short, but that's OK. We're doing the best we can.

Marybeth Hicks

College adventure begins with interview

"**R**ight this way, Katie," the admissions director says. In an instant, my daughter disappears down the hall, and just as quickly, her college adventure begins.

Of course, she doesn't head off to college for another year, so I suppose I'm indulging in a bit of maternal melodrama.

Nonetheless, my first baby, who it seems only minutes ago tried to climb out of the seat belt in the grocery cart to reach a forbidden bag of marshmallows, is walking into the office of a college admissions officer for a 30-minute interview.

More to the point, she is heading into the interview, and I am not.

There's no way I can nudge her to remember something outstanding she did in the past that might impress this man, no chance for me to correct her grammar or advise her to speak more slowly or to touch her hand gently to get her to stop fidgeting. She's really on her own, and short of an experience of mental telepathy (which I have never had), I can't communicate with her.

All I can do is hope and pray that nearly 17 years of parenting on the part of my husband and me will result in a conversation that reveals her good character, her humor and intellect and especially her decency and compassion.

I won't lie. I wish there were a way I could stand by the door and listen.

It occurs to me that my child is engaged in a discussion with someone whose perceptions might seal her fate. Suddenly, I realize that the whole college interview thing is a bit of a litmus test for quality parenting.

What if that little file the admissions director carried with him contains a checklist of vital observations that might make or break Katie's chances of getting into her school of choice?

Clean fingernails? Check.

Flossed teeth? Check.

Eye contact when speaking to an adult? Check.

Neurotic mother in the waiting room? Check.

Thankfully, I'm not alone. The admissions office is filled with nervous-looking moms and dads trying to appear relaxed as they flip through the pages of the college's brochures. We're all pretending to be reading about the wonderful opportunities our children will enjoy if they enroll here.

But really, we're wondering if our parenting will stand up to the scrutiny that goes beyond grade-point averages and test scores, reaching all the way to manners, ideas and philosophies.

No wonder we're all antsy.

The "half-hour interview" lasts more than an hour. When they return to the waiting area, Katie is chatting amiably with the admissions director, who turns and asks me, "Do you have any questions?"

I know he means "Do you have questions about the college?" I have only one question – How did she do? – which, of course, I don't ask.

Instead, we join a tour group, led by a current student who walks backward for more than an hour while taking us across the campus. Amazingly, he never trips or runs into traffic as he fills us in on college life.

We wander the grounds in a parent-child clump, listening carefully as our tour guide points out dormitories, classrooms, libraries and student centers.

He talks about faculty members and foreign-study programs and choosing a major.

He mentions that the library closes earlier on Friday and Saturday nights because the school encourages students to take time for socializing.

He tells us about cafeteria food and coffee shops. He even mentions a special program that lets students submit family recipes that can be prepared by the food service staff in case the student gets homesick for a favorite dish.

That's when it hits me. A year from now, her college choice will be made, and we'll be getting set to move our eldest child to her new home – a tiny room she'll share with another college freshman in a building full of 18-year-olds whose lives, like Katie's, will at last begin to take shape.

If the 12 months ahead are anything like the previous 16 years, I expect time will pass in an unwelcome flash, the days and weeks colliding in moments I can't capture or sometimes even recall.

Yet oddly, I'm wistful but not worried. Watching Katie absorb the campus tour, I realize she's projecting herself into a future that seems completely right, for which she will be completely ready.

I confess, the "melodrama mom" in me wants to whisper in her ear, "Just remember, sweetie, there's no place like home." But instead, I give her a smile and raise my eyebrows as if to say, "Cool place, huh?"

She smiles back, and it feels to me as if we have shared a whole conversation about leaving home and looking forward – in only a passing, knowing glance.

Thankfully, I still get a year with her before we start shopping for dorm accessories and shipping her off on her academic adventure. For now, her job is just to dream, to imagine what college will be like and to envision herself in a place that feels like home.

I just can't help but wonder what home will be like when she leaves.

Marybeth Hicks

Marybeth Hicks

Let the
boredom begin

Marybeth Hicks

Let the boredom begin

The call from the flute teacher comes at 8:05. The lesson was to have begun at 7:30. "We did it again," I yell up the stairs to my daughter. "It's Wednesday."

Suffice to say, this should not have come as a surprise. Wednesday began when I dragged myself out of bed in the morning for a full day of school and work, followed by soccer for my son, softball practice for one daughter and track practice for another, along with her weekly flute lesson in the evening.

I sheepishly apologize to the flute teacher for missing yet another lesson. It happens often enough that I no longer make excuses or do the "dance of confusion" for her. ("The lesson was today?") Thank goodness, she's too gracious to fire my daughter from her roster of high-school musicians, so I get my calendar, and we look for another opening.

That we are overbooked is obvious. The calendar on the refrigerator posts cryptic reminders of various activities for every member of the family, including the dog. If we could read them all, we might be more organized.

When my children were small, I wondered about families that operated like whole groups of Energizer bunnies, running here and there in an endless sprint to lessons, rehearsals, practices and games.

Smugly, I held my toddlers on my hips and smiled the knowing smile of a "woman who would do it differently." I would say "no" to the fast pace that robs families of unity and cohesiveness and dinners on weeknights.

Fat chance. I had about as much hope of avoiding a busy schedule as I had of avoiding trips to the grocery store with barefooted, filth-covered, sticky children in pajamas. (I said I would never do that, either.) From the safe distance of inexperience, I thought the lifestyle we would enjoy was a choice I could make.

In reality, commitments simply appear on your agenda like so many dust bunnies in the corners of your house that you have no time to clean because you're always driving someone to a game.

Like every family I know, we are ruled by our calendar. The particulars may vary, but the atmosphere in most suburban homes is roughly the same. My children take music lessons and dance class; they belong to the band (after-school practice), the media team (early morning arrival) and the French club. (When it meets, we must send food.)

Cross-country season becomes the spring musical which becomes track season. My children play basketball, basketball and more basketball, peppering the week with practices, games, tournaments – team party? "Sure. We'll host," I'm likely to say.

The breathless juggling of activities culminates every year in May – a month I am grateful to say is over. With four children, the month of May is not the coming of spring but a punishing ritual perpetrated by schools on unsuspecting parents.

It's a marathon of choral concerts, awards ceremonies, fine-arts exhibits, field trips and group projects. It's the mad dash to the finish line of the academic year.

The conspiracy theorist in me can't help but suspect the hectic haze of May is designed by the educational establishment to perpetuate the now-unnecessary agricultural school year.

Seriously – how many of us really need our children home all summer for the harvest? Wouldn't our tax and tuition dollars go further if school buildings didn't sit dormant for three months? But a 12-month academic year would eliminate summers off for teachers – and that's where my theory comes into play.

I think the overextended scheduling in May creates in us parents the willingness to keep our children home for 12 relentless weeks of summer, the second day of which will begin with the sound of one of our offspring whining, "I'm bored."

Of course, the reason they're bored is they have been overprogrammed and overstimulated for at least the past month. When your child is accustomed to 16-hour days packed with school, homework, extracurricular activities and the odd orthodontist appointment, a few consecutive days of rest and relaxation feel like Earth has stopped spinning.

It's good for children to be a little bored. Boredom is the reason for lemonade stands and sidewalk chalk and daydreaming. But summer isn't what it used to be – a time for hammocks and bike rides and trips to the ice-cream shop after dinner, as much as I wish it were.

According to my calendar, now computerized with color codes and categories to reduce the chance of missing anything, summer looks a lot like the rest of the year. Between drama camp, running camp, basketball camp and cheerleading camp are activities planned to keep each child busy for at least a week or two.

Then again, when I scroll down my high-tech family planner into the dog days of summer, it looks as if there's room for a picnic in the park and maybe a drive to the lake. I might just block out the time for those now, in case something else comes up and we get too busy to be bored.

Marybeth Hicks

Parenting in a poolside petri dish

I f I ever get a Ph.D. in parenting, I know where I'll go to do my research: a hotel pool. A hotel pool is a microcosm of parenting styles – a virtual petri dish where one may observe a host of child-rearing tactics.

My doctoral thesis would begin with the observation that poolside parenting is inherently difficult. This is because it offers the delusion that an adult will engage in an activity that is fun and relaxing.

Such an adult – say, a mom – may come to the pool for a pleasant visit with a friend. If she is alone, she may bring a book or a magazine to the pool with the intent of reading quietly while her children swim and play.

She has her SPF 4 sunscreen – a no no for the children – which she'll slather on just before closing her eyes, spreading her fingers and toes, and drifting off on a coconut-scented dream.

Parents who do this are the people whose children run amok under the watch-ful, if not irritated, eyes of the non-visiting, non-reading, non-snoozing adults on the chairs nearby.

My thesis would include several case studies of this phenomenon, such as the ones I observed this week while on a family vacation. I'm positioned within splash-ing distance of the hotel pool, angled toward both the water and the sun, when two mothers stroll onto the pool deck.

Bounding around these mothers are two boys around the age of 10. One mom pushes her sleeping baby in a stroller (the kind in which an entire preschool could be transported).

The boys drop their towels, jump out of their sandals and grab their swim goggles, quickly heading toward the cool, refreshing waters of the pool.

The moms rearrange their chairs around an umbrella table, put the baby in a shady spot, organize their sunscreen bottles and diet sodas, and sit down for a chat. One of them positions her back to the pool, establishing the validity of my doctoral hypothesis: Some parents come to the pool to let others supervise their children.

Before long, the boys climb out of the pool and jump in again and again and again. Now they run and jump. Now one boy says, "Let's run and dive in at the same time," which they do – into the pool's greatest depth, which is 5 feet. Let's say that again for emphasis: the pool's greatest depth, which is 5 feet.

Betsy emerges from the pool and approaches me to ask a question, standing close enough to me that the drips from her sopping-wet frame land on my warm, dry body, which is another reason adults can't really enjoy going to the pool.

I use the opportunity to warn my daughter (and admonish the divers because I'm deliberately too loud), "Did you see those kids diving into the pool? Don't ever do that. It's totally unsafe, and diving is against the pool rules."

When it looks as if the boys are getting ready for another death-defying dive into the shallow waters of stupidity, I speak up (loudly enough so their mothers could hear if they weren't engaged in such an animated conversation), "Honey, you can't do that. It's very unsafe, and the rules say 'no diving.'" I point to the rules at the side of the pool for effect.

One boy glances back with a face that recalls Robert De Niro in the movie *Taxi Driver* and the cinematic classic, "You talkin' to me?"

Then, proving he has no respect for authority (I cited the pool rules, for heaven's sake), he runs (not walks) to the far side of the pool and dives head first into the water directly over the words "Three Feet." Lucky for him, he's short.

I watch him surface, apparently unscathed, and then decide our swimming time conveniently is over. I don't want to stick around long enough for the accident that most certainly is waiting to happen.

Of course, even if the mother of this aquatic daredevil had been paying attention and had asserted herself to enforce some basic rules of safety, there's a good chance this boy might not have complied. That's because earlier in his young life she might have employed the parenting style I observed in the management of little Adrianna, a hotel pool guest of about 24 months.

Adrianna – a name her parents and grandparents repeated no fewer than 462 times (but who's counting?) as in, "Adrianna, do you want your duckie?" and "Adrianna, splash the water" and "Adrianna, say 'cheese!'" and "Adrianna, isn't Daddy silly?"

Adrianna, Adrianna, Adrianna. This little girl may have issues later in life, but I doubt she'll have an identity crisis.

Mostly, her loving family used Adrianna's name while trying to coax her away from the pool when it was time to go.

"Adrianna, let's get ice cream."

"Adrianna, sit with Nanny."

"Adrianna, here's your toy."

Those four adults tried everything they could think of to stop Adrianna from stubbornly returning to the edge of the pool, holding tight to her Minnie Mouse floatie.

The only thing they didn't try was "Adrianna, no more swimming."

Instead, when all the coaxing and pleading clearly wasn't working, Adrianna's dad got back into the pool, Adrianna's mother handed her over to him, and off she drifted to the cooing sound of "Motorboat, motorboat, go so slow."

I don't think I'll ever get that doctorate, but if I do, I'm getting a lifeguard whistle first.

Marybeth Hicks

Bickering just part of group dynamic

When school let out, I was excited about summer, but that's because I had forgotten about the bickering.

With four children at home, bickering among my youngsters obviously is a year-round issue. Nevertheless, the high season for bickering is late summer, coincidental with the "dog days," when tempers and temperatures generally flare and three months of togetherness wears like sand in your swimsuit.

On any given morning, bickering ensues before breakfast with a meaningless debate about who gets "the good chair" to watch cartoons.

Then it's a quick tussle over the morning meal – who got the last "everything" bagel and which lucky sibling gets the remaining Lucky Charms.

When I assign kitchen chores (this isn't exactly heavy labor – just unloading and reloading the dishwasher), sparks fly over who had this job yesterday and the day before and who will do it tomorrow and next Tuesday.

There's a rule about bickering: The intensity of the argument increases disproportionately with the importance of the subject. Ergo, the topic that causes the most vitriolic – albeit empty – bickering is about the seating arrangement in the van. Seriously.

Anyone with more than one child knows what I mean.

Who sits where in the van has consumed more emotional energy than all subjects of debate combined – and with literally a hundred opportunities each week to jockey for position, I might listen to bickering over this nonissue up to a dozen times a day.

Like now, for instance. I'm sitting here with the motor running, adjusting the rearview mirror while waiting for the gang to appear in bathing suits and flip-flops for a trip to the pool. There's room for one child in the front passenger seat, two in the middle section and a fourth in "the way back."

Because it's just a 10-minute drive, the fighting will be particularly fierce.

One by one, they trickle out of the house and into the garage, past the shoe baskets where the flip-flops should be (but usually aren't – a topic for another day) and into the van. The rule is that the first one in goes to "the way back." It seemed like a logical rule when I made it. We would fill the car from the rear to avoid crawling over the other passengers – but this is the reason nobody wants to be the first one in, which probably also is why I'm sitting in an empty van.

As often happens, my children ignore the rule. One of the older girls gets in front, and the next two out of the house occupy the captain's chairs in the center of the van. The last one out is miffed, thinking she had waited long enough to get one of the "good seats." She begins her offensive with that trusty opener, "They always sit in the middle."

By now, I'm tired of waiting and even more impatient with the incessant arguing, so I don't enforce the "way back" rule. Instead, I apply arbitrary parental problem solving to stop the volley of snippy remarks. "Hey, you snooze, you lose." With that, we're off to the pool.

Once, in an effort to curb the conflicts, I tried assigned seats. It lasted about a week because I couldn't remember who was supposed to sit where and when I had said I would rotate the assignments.

Besides, I've come to realize that for siblings, bickering actually is a form of bonding. Face it, they're not about to engage in some hokey made-for-TV sibling lovefest (think *The Brady Bunch* forming a band). So instead, they foster an intense emotional bond by shooting each other dirty looks and sneers.

By the time we reach the pool and stake out a few lounge chairs, my tolerance for testiness has reached an end. When Katie and Betsy exchange caustic comments over possession of a chair, I declare an end to all sibling communication. "One more nasty exchange and we're going home." (And thanks for spoiling my happy mood – but I don't say this.)

They look at me in stunned disbelief. "Mom – we're just kidding with each other. Lighten up."

Just kidding? How am I supposed to tell the jokes from the loathful disdain? It all sounds the same to me.

Sure enough, in a matter of minutes, all four of my children are in the pool, splashing and swimming together. The tension and irritability from the van seem to have dissolved in the cool blue water. I have no idea why they suddenly are friends again, but I'm not complaining.

In my dreams, they never would fuss about insignificant issues such as seating arrangements in the van. They would just pile in, grateful that we have a van – not to mention that it is piloted by a driver who takes them everywhere they need to go.

They would offer the rest of the Oreo-cookie ice cream to each other instead of fighting over it until it melts.

They would say things like, "Could you move over a little?" while walking in the mall instead of, "Get out of my way" as if they have encountered a cockroach.

They even would realize that most of their fights could be avoided with the simple exercise of manners and courtesy.

In short, they would treat each other like strangers instead of siblings.

Then again, without all their bickering, they wouldn't be so close, would they?

Marybeth Hicks

Family loves the dog days of summer

I t's the first day of summer vacation, so I expected him to sleep late, but this is ridiculous. He's sprawled over the bed like a sailor sleeping off a two-day bender, and he hasn't flinched. In fact, when I checked on him, he was so still I had to watch carefully to see if he was breathing.

His exhaustion shouldn't surprise me. Last night he roamed the neighborhood until darkness finally descended over the yard. I suppose it was disorienting to hear the sounds of children playing as night fell, and he just couldn't bring himself to call it quits and come inside.

Already, his reliable routine is upended, with people coming and going at all hours of the day. The regular rhythm of the school year has been replaced with slamming doors, strangers in the driveway and telephones that ring incessantly.

Summertime may be the season for lazy, hazy days, but so far, all the activity and noise of having four children around the house is confusing my dog.

Scotty is a 30-pound "Daisy dog," a canine cocktail that used to be known as a mutt. We got him on the advice of our pediatrician because he's hypo-allergenic – his heritage as part bichon frise, part shih tzu and part poodle eliminate the health and housekeeping hassles of having a dog that sheds. These fluffy, likable pups usually grow to about 12 or 14 pounds, but we wanted a larger version that could withstand the affection of four boisterous youngsters.

Dogs are pack animals, of course, and Scotty clearly loves belonging to the Hicks family pack. He rightly has identified me as the alpha human in the house, being as I'm the one who returns from the hunt with those big green bags of dog chow. For this reason, no matter how many people are home, I am the center of our dog's universe.

From the day we got Scotty, more than five years ago, he has followed me from room to room to remain within six feet of my loving, if not benign, supervision. Quite honestly, it's annoying – made all the more so by the fact that several members of the family long to be the object of his devotion, and they accuse me of ingratitude. Easy for them to say; I'm the one who nearly trips over the beast several times a day.

Still, Scotty and I have an understanding. I make sure that his needs are met, his coat is groomed and his legal status is maintained; he lets me know when the UPS delivery truck arrives.

We're creatures of habit. We enjoy a daily pattern that includes time for housework, desk work, errands, cooking and carpooling (my list) and sleeping (his list). In unspoken familiarity, we follow our weekday pattern with precision from the first of September, when the school bell rings in the "new year," through early June, when report cards signal the completion of another academic cycle.

For roughly nine months, we enjoy the peace and productivity that comes only in a quiet house, but now that summer vacation has begun, we're both a little out of sorts.

The difference between Scotty and me is that he can continue to accomplish the thing on his "to do" list, while I face a daily challenge to complete my tasks.

I'll make countless trips to the local pool with a cooler of sandwiches and a file of work, but Scotty will nap by the front door.

The laundry will pile up in heaps next to the washer because of frequent apparel changes throughout every summer day, but Scotty will retire to his favorite spot under the divan.

I'll clean the kitchen seven times before noon while simultaneously calling doctors and dentists to schedule summer checkups; Scotty will escape to the chair in the den and flip himself over in a posture that says, "Wake me only if you promise to scratch me."

The only real difference in Scotty's life is the increased opportunity to bolt out of the house via one of many doors left open by careless children. When this happens, he'll trot jauntily down the center of our street, looking left and right for the person who facilitated his freedom, hoping for a quick game of chase.

He's a great dog, really. I sometimes complain about him, but in truth, he's the pet I always dreamed of having as a young girl, when my parents refused to get a dog for me on the grounds I had five siblings and therefore plenty of playmates.

When my husband was growing up, his family always had dogs – hunting dogs, in fact. Jim envisioned a similar animal for our children, a gallant, regal canine with skills and a name like Champ or Rex or Prince.

Instead, we got a dog whose formal moniker is Butterscotch, a name he doesn't recognize as his own. He has few skills, he won't come when he's called, but at least he doesn't make any of us sneeze.

He's the perfect pet for the Hicks pack, and now that it's summer, my children are all enjoying the extra dog days.

Then again, when summer's over, my dog days will just be returning. Woof.

Marybeth Hicks

Marking history helps dad teach values

Great gray clouds drift overhead as a stiff September breeze blows unexpectedly cold air through the holes of my cable-knit sweater.

Standing in the middle of a former Canadian battlefield known as the Plains of Abraham, I am learning more than just the history of the French people who came to Quebec.

I'm learning something I didn't know about my husband, Jim: He reads historical markers – all of them, every word.

It's a habit I hadn't noticed before, or if I did, love blinded me to what this would mean in the years to come.

Now, though, hopping from foot to foot on the sidewalk while the whipping wind slaps my hair into my squinting eyes, I realize this is my destiny from now until eternity. I have vowed to stand with my hands in my pockets, shoulders scrunched to my ears in the posture of one underdressed for the weather, and wait for the man of my dreams to absorb not only the facts that recount the history of a particular place, but its aura, its atmosphere.

He reads. He scans. He transports himself backward in time to imagine what it was like to be here when something significant was happening – something that would merit a marker to be read by future generations.

When finally he grasps the awesome size and scope of the battle explained in bronze and affixed to the side of one rock or another, he shakes his head in appreciation, looks at me as if rediscovering the era in which he actually lives, and says, "Ready?"

This sliver of discovery occurred almost 20 years ago when, on a newlywed jaunt to the lovely French-Canadian province of Quebec, I observed the "historical marker thing."

It was a surprise to me all those years ago that anyone actually would read all the plaques and signs posted in a park or along a highway, but by now, I'm used to it.

Jim loves history, a subject that plays to his exceptional memory. He's one who subscribes to 19th-century philosopher George Santayana's belief that "those who cannot remember the past are condemned to repeat it." So in addition to being fascinated by historical stories and events, he thinks it's important to recall what he learns.

Because I can't remember what happened last Tuesday, much less on a Tuesday in 1834, I'm not a huge history buff.

For me, history is a *Jeopardy!* category I would avoid in favor of Insects or Kevin Costner Movie Roles. This is why I'm not a person who lingers at historical markers. (There's a credible case to be made for the reverse logic, but no matter.)

A nominal aptitude for history (and an embarrassing lack of interest) not withstanding, I have found as a parent that the "historical marker thing" comes in handy. If you see one, and your children don't notice it right away, you can bone up quickly on tidbits of information to convince your offspring you are all-knowing.

Unfortunately, this only works well when children are young. As mine got a bit older, they figured out that I'm usually not able to offer any greater detail than is conveyed on the marker itself, leading them to conclude that my knowledge base is scant, if not highly selective.

On the other hand, ask any question about history, and Dad will have the answer.

Not just the facts, but the context, the political flavor, the cultural significance. He's the *Encyclopaedia Britannica* of dads, our own personal Google search engine.

I confess that earlier in our marriage, I didn't appreciate this about Jim, what with all the waiting in brutal cold and excessive heat while he read historical markers to add to his remarkable storehouse of dates and data.

But Jim makes the past interesting to our children, and consequently, I'm surrounded by five people whose regular dinner-table conversation might include observations about the American Revolution or the fall of Rome or the building of the Great Wall of China – and not just events in history, but people.

His ability to make history interesting to our children helps them understand the connection between events of the past and the circumstances of our world today.

The cool thing about watching Jim share what he knows is that he teaches our children so much more than just the stories of a world gone by. He teaches them about what he values.

When he talks to them about Thomas Jefferson or Abraham Lincoln or Winston Churchill or Rosa Parks, he teaches our children not only about people whose determination and courage marked the time in which they lived, but about the qualities of good character their father admires and emulates.

These days, history is measured in generations, not eras. We name our decades as if slapping on a label gives a period of just 10 years lasting significance – as though epic proportions could ever be construed by a name such as "the Me Generation."

Historians like Jim understand that history unfolds slowly and that learning about the past is a crucial way to teach the next generation the values that might lead them to future greatness.

Fortunately for those of us who don't remember all the events in history we should, there are markers almost everywhere we go.

Marybeth Hicks

Just a day at the (nude) beach

O K, so the truth is we actually walked the beach looking for the naked people. But let me explain.

Our day at the ocean finds our friends from Michigan joining us for a day of surf, sand and sun at Robert Moses State Park on Long Island's south shore. We set up beach chairs, towels and toys and head down to jump the waves.

The teenaged girls in our entourage set out to scope the landscape. They return with some startling news: There are nude sunbathers down the beach.

Actual naked people.

"No way!" we all respond. I ask my husband, the Native New Yorker, if it's possible there is a nude beach at a public park. He says probably not an officially sanctioned nude beach, but if people disrobe and lather sunscreen over the family jewels in a remote section of the park, nobody's going to make much of a fuss. "This is New York, after all," he says in a condescending tone – implying, "Remember I'm the one who hails from the cultural and intellectual Center of the Universe."

About this time, my girlfriend – we'll call her "Annie" – and I decide a break is in order from our maternal hovering. We let the dads hold back the encroaching undertow and count heads while we take a power walk along the shore.

A few steps into our walk, Annie's 10-year-old son – we'll call him "Grady" – asks to join us. Since we're pretty sure the report of public nudity is a hoax, Annie says "sure" and we trek down the surf line, our footsteps disappearing behind us.

We pass the "boogie board zone," an area populated by guys named Vinnie and Anthony wearing board shorts and those expensive nylon shirts that accentuate a Gold's Gym physique.

Now comes the unguarded beach, the "no swim zone." Right away, the population of sunbathers thins to an anti-social few. These are the serious readers who wouldn't notice if the incoming tide rolled over their heads and left clams in their hair.

And then, nobody. Bare beach, so to speak. Grady complains the walk is too long and lobbies to turn around. I tell him we're only going as far as the lighthouse (about three miles away). He tries to defect, but Annie won't let him walk alone back to our spot.

About this time, we see a park police SUV cruising the sand. Annie thinks this is odd so we follow its trail with our gaze, only to land our collective stare on its destination – a wrinkled, sagging, naked couple. They have to be at least 60. They may think they're getting a "St. Tropez tan" but it's more like "Sand Toupee."

The SUV pulls up next to them and the park policeman talks through his open window. The topless woman stays put, but her male companion – wearing only a sleeveless t-shirt (what's the point of that?) arises out of his lounge chair and heads toward the parking lot. His bare behind peeks from below the hem. Thank heaven he's not walking toward us.

The SUV makes its way further down the sand and we realize this is an entire colony of what appear to be aging hippies attired in the altogether. They're bronzed, they're proud, and say it out loud – they're buck nekkid! The officer stops to talk shortly with various nudies who appear to argue their cases, whereafter the men shake the sand from their exposed parts and jiggle their way up to the parking lot.

We gawk for all of 60 seconds, during which Annie shields Grady's eyes as we giggle like the middle-aged Midwestern moms we are. We head back to our beach chairs speculating on the conversation in the park police station. "Bill, it's your turn to go out and tell the nudies to cover up their privates…" "Not me, Sarge! I had nudie duty last weekend!"

Grady decides this episode will make a great essay for the inevitable fifth grade assignment, "How I Spent My Summer Vacation." He composes his account on our return walk, dodging sandcastles as he captures the experience. "Last summer, our friends took us to a nude beach in New York and we had a great time." Through the eyes of a ten-year-old, public nudity is even more entertaining than passing gas.

Back at our beach chairs, I look around at the miles of exposed skin. Ironically, I'm thankful for the strings that pass for bikinis on the thousands of girls named Angela all around us. It's sure not modest, but it could be worse.

Marybeth Hicks

Again with the naked people!

This is for the woman at the beach in South Florida swimming roughly 10 yards from my 11-year-old son: For heaven's sake, put on some clothes.

I'm not advocating something out of the ordinary, such as a full-length diver's suit. Heck, I would be happy with the same standard of modesty exhibited by Eve after the incident with the apple and the serpent. Even a fig leaf would have spared Jimmy the embarrassment of swimming near a bona fide exhibitionist.

Is it unreasonable to expect my fellow beach-goers to cover their most personal body parts, especially in the presence of families with young children, like mine?

Am I a prude?

There we were, eking out the last hours of our vacation before heading to the airport, soaking in what little sun was peeking through the billowing rain clouds.

Never mind that the wind was picking up. We were running out of time. I wrapped myself in a stray T-shirt belonging to one of my children and pretended the sun's ultraviolet rays really were penetrating my skin.

My husband and I sat close together on a beach towel and watched our children bob in the surf. They didn't mind the iffy weather, as it created some chop in the water, resulting in waves they could ride to shore.

Despite the threatening skies, it was an idyllic "last day of vacation." We had stockpiled a week's worth of memories, and Jim and I talked quietly, savoring bits and pieces of the trip.

That's when the naked lady decided to go for a swim.

To be fair, it's not accurate to say she was naked, because nudity is defined as a complete lack of clothing. This woman had a small piece of fabric tied with strings where a bikini bottom should have been, but that was it.

Nevertheless, the water beckoned her, not lazily but urgently. This gal needed a swim something fierce – either that or she's just one of those people who "dives right in" to any situation – so she didn't saunter to the surf and put a toe in the water.

She bounded and bounced her way over the waves, right next to my four unsuspecting children. Talk about making a splash.

Maybe in South Florida beach communities, people are more cosmopolitan than we suburban types, but I confess I was shocked to see more than a few women sporting the European swimsuit (bottom; no top). It's not something you find at the local community swimming pool, or at least not where I live.

Thankfully, because the water was warmer than the air, the topless (and essentially bottomless) swimmer stayed mostly underwater.

Jim and I sat in disbelief. I suspect we were awed for different reasons, but I'm giving my husband the benefit of the doubt. He's a good and faithful spouse, after all, so I assume his jaw dropped for the same morally upright reasons mine did.

We decided not to call attention to her on the off chance the children hadn't noticed the fleshy figure hopping the waves next to them. But let's face it, nude strangers are hard to miss.

To be clear, this wasn't an area of the beach designated for nude sunbathing. And ours wasn't the only family out for a Sunday afternoon swim; there were children everywhere.

If we were in a locale where this was the custom, I at least would have had the chance to prepare my children for what they might see. I even tried to listen for broken English or a foreign language in the hope that the woman's partial nudity reflected some other cultural tradition, albeit an immodest one.

No go. This woman was as American as apple pie.

To their credit, my son and daughters pretended not to notice her. After a while, the strength of the current transported the woman farther down the shore, while I insisted that my children swim safely in front of my husband and me.

When they got out of the water, however, they had questions

"Did you see that woman?" one daughter asked.

"Is that legal?" another daughter wondered.

I figured my son would be curious, too, and sure enough, he had a question: "Can we get ice cream?"

You have to love an 11-year-old.

Obviously, Jimmy knows it's inappropriate for a woman to be unclothed in public. He lives in a house full of girls who slam doors when he walks past, and he took the introduction to health class. He gets it.

It's not that he failed to notice; he simply chose to reduce the embarrassment of the whole situation by ignoring it.

Turns out Jimmy made a point, even if he didn't mean to do so. If we all withheld our attention from exhibitionists such as the lady on the beach ("lady" being a word I'm using liberally), there might be less incentive to parade around in the altogether. It's the attention that makes it so appealing to act outside the norms of social convention, and these days, you won't get much attention on a beach simply wearing a bikini.

Then again, there's another reason to look the other way: By pretending he didn't see her, my young son afforded that woman the modesty she would not afford herself.

By undressing in public, she chose to dishonor her dignity, but my son didn't.

Sadly, the fact that he was more concerned about it than she was is even more embarrassing than swimming in the buff.

Marybeth Hicks

On vacation with my stalker

I t's vacation time. Our trek across the fruited plain includes a Saturday night stop in the heartland, where we awaken to hunt down an eight o'clock Mass and a diner for breakfast.

We don't know the way from the hotel to the nearest Catholic church, and when we find it, Mass has started and we're late.

We stand in the back and wait to slip, unnoticed, into a pew. Of course, this is physically impossible. There are six of us wearing travel clothes and squeaky rubber sneakers. Our sheepish faces say, "You don't know us but we're The Late Family. We don't really belong here. You'll never see us again so please forgive the disturbance."

We slide into an empty pew as the congregation sings the psalm. As the Gospel reading begins, we focus our attention on the priest, as well as on the ornate ceilings and beautiful frescoes painted high above our heads.

And then, my Stalker strikes.

That's right, Stalker. I'm being stalked by a small child who distracts my every heavenly thought by talking, screaming, crying and fussing through virtually any religious service I attend.

And here I am on vacation, just passing through Ohio. And she's standing on the kneeler behind me, squealing "Wummer duckie! Wummer duckie!" over and over and over again.

Her Cheerios litter the floor and bounce under my pew. When I stand up, I will crush them and later, track them up the center aisle.

My Stalker has cast a spell over the adults in her family. They think the sound of her new vocabulary bouncing off the frescoed ceiling is engaging. Amazing. Really cute.

They're consumed with the extraordinary fun of whispering "rubber ducky" and hearing her parroted reply, decibels louder and sweeter: "Wummer duckie!"

They smile and snuggle and coo. Apparently, they think they're alone in this building. She's good, and she knows it.

I'm fuming. My eyes roll upward, my shoulders tense, and my breathing converts to the controlled sighs of The Truly Honked Off.

And then, I hear God's call.

Actually, it was my mother, on my cell phone, which I never would have dreamed in a million years I had left on, while traveling across country, and why is she calling me at 8:20 on a Sunday morning? I'm flustered beyond belief.

Where is the damn phone?

Buried under the wallet, the lipstick, someone's asthma inhaler, my sunglasses, which are now caught on the phone, which if I don't grab just right I will not silence but will inadvertently answer, and she'll probably call back thinking we were disconnected before I have a chance to disable the "key guard" feature, enable the "silent" mode and then turn it off without hearing that annoying, "da-da-dah-dah-dah" song.

Yes, it was God, disguised as my mother on a cell phone, calling to remind me that the fussy baby once was mine.

He was calling to flash a mental image of my own kids crying in church, before they could respond to the words: "Stop crying;" calling to reminisce about longing to stay in the Sanctuary and not pace the vestibule, where the acoustics are bad and the air is cold.

Calling to say, "Hey you – Mrs. Late Family – lighten up. Those people are showered and dressed and they got here before you did. You should know how hard that was to accomplish."

Boy, did he have a lot to say in that one little call.

Most of the time when God calls it's subtle. I need the gift of discernment to even know it was He, and for sure to understand what the heck He wants. This time, however, I was on His speed dial.

OK, so I wish He would also call my Stalker's parents and explain the concept of bailing until after the homily so the congregation can concentrate.

But I guess, as usual, that's his call, not mine

Marybeth Hicks